Simple & Sensational

RECIPES

Publications International, Ltd.

Favorite Brand Name Recipes at www.fbnr.com

Nutritional Analysis: Every effort has been made to check the accuracy of the nutritional information that appears with each recipe. However, because numerous variables account for a wide range of values for certain foods, nutritive analyses in this book should be considered approximate. Different results may be obtained by using different nutrient databases and different brand-name products.

Microwave Cooking: Microwave ovens vary in wattage. Use the cooking times as guidelines and check for doneness before adding more time.

Preparation/Cooking Times: Preparation times are based on the approximate amount of time required to assemble the recipe before cooking, baking, chilling or serving. These times include preparation steps such as measuring, chopping and mixing. The fact that some preparations and cooking can be done simultaneously is taken into account. Preparation of optional ingredients and serving suggestions is not included.

contents

**Look for the
QUICK & EASY ICON
on recipes that will make
you a hit in a hurry!**

Breakfast and Brunch

French Toast Strata

Prep Time:
15 minutes

Cook Time:
50 minutes

Total Time:
9 hours

**Makes
8 servings**

⅓ cup **SPLENDA®** No Calorie Sweetener, Granulated

1 cup **egg substitute**

⅔ cup **skim milk**

¾ teaspoon **imitation maple flavor**

8 slices **cinnamon-raisin bread**

2 cups **peeled apples, thinly sliced**

¼ cup **low fat cream cheese**

1 tablespoon **SPLENDA®** No Calorie Sweetener, Granulated

½ teaspoon **cinnamon**

1. Preheat oven to 350°F. Spray an 8-inch square cake pan with nonstick cooking spray. Set aside.

2. Blend together ⅓ cup SPLENDA® Granulated Sweetener, egg substitute, milk, and maple flavor in a medium bowl.

3. Tear cinnamon-raisin bread into pieces, approximately 1–2 inches each. Add bread and sliced apples into mixing bowl with other ingredients. Toss to coat bread. Pour bread mixture into prepared pan.

4. Cut cream cheese into 8 chunks and place on top of strata.

5. Blend remaining 1 tablespoon SPLENDA® Granulated Sweetener and cinnamon together. Sprinkle over strata. Cover and refrigerate overnight.

6. Bake in the preheated oven 40–50 minutes, or until lightly browned and set. Serve immediately.

Per serving: calories 150 (calories from fat 35), protein 8g, fat 4g (saturated fat 1g), carbohydrates 21g, fiber 2g, cholesterol 5mg, sodium 200mg, sugar 11g
Dietary exchanges: 1½ starches, 1 fat

Breakfast Trifle

Prep Time:
25 minutes

Total Time:
2 hours,
25 minutes

**Makes
10 servings**

½ **cup SPLENDA® No Calorie Sweetener, Granulated**

4 **cups plain nonfat yogurt**

2 **teaspoons vanilla extract**

9 **slices Italian style or other white bread, crusts removed**

12 **ounces frozen unsweetened raspberries, thawed**

2 **tablespoons SPLENDA® No Calorie Sweetener, Granulated**

1 **(15-ounce) can cling peaches, no sugar added, drained**

16 **ounces frozen dark pitted sweet cherries, thawed and drained**

1 **banana, thinly sliced**

1. Blend ½ cup of SPLENDA® Granulated Sweetener, plain yogurt, and vanilla together in a medium mixing bowl. Set aside.

2. Cut bread into rectangles.

3. Mix together raspberries and 2 tablespoons SPLENDA® Granulated Sweetener gently. Do not drain raspberries.

4. To assemble trifle: Pour ½ cup of yogurt mixture in the bottom of the glass bowl.

5 Place ⅓ of the sliced bread on top of the yogurt mixture. Top bread with ⅓ of the peaches, ⅓ of the cherries and ⅓ of the raspberries. Drizzle about ⅓ of the raspberry juice onto the bread.

6. Place ⅓ of the thinly sliced banana on top of the raspberries. Pour ⅓ of the yogurt mixture over the bread and fruit.

7. Repeat steps 5–6 two more times, ending by pouring the remaining yogurt over the fruit.

8. Cover and refrigerate at least 2 hours or overnight, allowing the bread to fully absorb the fruit juices.

Per serving: calories 200 (calories from fat 10), protein 8g, fat 1g (saturated fat 0g), carbohydrates 39g, fiber 3g, cholesterol 0mg, sodium 190mg, sugar 17g
Dietary exchanges: 1 starch, 1 fruit, ½ fat-free milk

Pistachio Cranberry Scones

Prep Time:
10 minutes

Cook Time:
15 minutes

Total Time:
25 minutes

**Makes
14 servings**

3 cups all-purpose flour

1½ teaspoons cream of tartar

¾ teaspoon baking soda

½ teaspoon salt

1 tablespoon orange zest

6 tablespoons butter

⅓ cup SPLENDA® No Calorie Sweetener, Granulated

¾ cup 1% low-fat milk

½ cup dried cranberries

½ cup chopped pistachio nuts

1. Preheat oven to 425°F. Spray a cookie sheet with nonstick cooking spray.

2. Combine flour, cream of tartar, soda, salt, and orange zest in a large bowl; cut in butter with a pastry blender until mixture is crumbly. Add SPLENDA® Granulated Sweetener and milk to dry ingredients, stirring just until dry ingredients are moistened. Stir in cranberries and pistachio nuts.

3. Pat dough to a ¾-inch thickness on a lightly floured surface. Cut scones with a 2½-inch round biscuit cutter, and place on cookie sheet.

4. Bake for 12–15 minutes or until lightly browned.

Per serving: calories 190 (calories from fat 70), protein 4g, fat 7g (saturated fat 3g), carbohydrates 26g, fiber 2g, cholesterol 15mg, sodium 230mg, sugar 4g
Dietary exchanges: 2 starches, 1 fat

Pumpkin Waffles

Prep Time:
15 minutes

Cook Time:
5 minutes

Total Time:
20 minutes

**Makes
6 servings**

1 cup all-purpose flour

1 teaspoon baking powder

½ teaspoon baking soda

¼ teaspoon salt

¾ teaspoon ground cinnamon

½ teaspoon ground ginger

⅛ teaspoon ground nutmeg

2 teaspoons canola oil

1 teaspoon molasses

¼ cup canned pumpkin

1 cup buttermilk

1 large egg

2 tablespoons SPLENDA® No Calorie Sweetener, Granulated

1½ cups maple syrup sweetened with SPLENDA® Brand Sweetener

1. Preheat waffle iron according to manufacturer's directions; spray lightly with nonstick cooking spray.

2. Combine flour, baking powder, soda, salt, cinnamon, ginger, and nutmeg in a large bowl. Set aside.

3. Combine oil, molasses, pumpkin, and buttermilk in a small bowl; set aside.

4. Whisk together egg and SPLENDA® Granulated Sweetener until blended. Add buttermilk mixture, whisking until blended. Add to dry ingredients, stirring just until moistened.

5. Pour batter into a hot waffle iron and bake approximately 5 minutes.* Serve with maple syrup.

*Follow manufacturer's directions for bake times.

Per serving: calories 160 (calories from fat 25), protein 5g, fat 3g (saturated fat 1g), carbohydrates 32g, fiber 1g, cholesterol 35mg, sodium 400mg, sugar 3g
Dietary exchanges: 2 starches, ½ fat

Pomegranate Jelly

Prep Time:
45 minutes

Cook Time:
8 minutes

Total Time:
53 minutes

**Makes
48 servings**

4 cups bottled pomegranate juice

1 (1.75 ounce) package low methoxyl pectin with calcium

1½ cups SPLENDA® No Calorie Sweetener, Granulated

1. Wash jars and lids in hot soapy water; rinse with warm water. Fill boiling-water canner half full with water; add jars and water to cover. Bring water to a boil, reduce heat and simmer. Place lids in water to cover in a small saucepan; bring water to a simmer. Simmer until ready to use. Remove and drain jars and lids, one at a time, as needed for filling.

2. Combine pomegranate juice and pectin in a large saucepan; stirring until pectin dissolves. Let stand 10 minutes.

3. Bring pomegranate juice mixture to a full rolling boil (a boil that doesn't stop bubbling when stirred) over medium-high heat. Skim off any foam with metal spoon. Boil for 1 minute, stirring constantly. Remove from heat; add SPLENDA® Granulated Sweetener stirring until SPLENDA® Granulated Sweetener dissolves. Skim off any foam with metal spoon.

4. Ladle hot jelly immediately into prepared jars, filling to within ¼ inch of tops. Wipe jar rims and threads. Cover with 2-piece lids. Screw bands tightly. Place jars on elevated rack in canner. Lower rack into canner. (Water must cover jars by 1–2 inches. Add boiling water, if necessary.) Cover; bring water to gentle boil.

5. Process 10 minutes. Remove jars and place upright on towel to cool completely. After jars cool, check seals by pressing center of lid with finger. (If lid springs back, lid is not sealed and refrigeration is necessary.) Store in a cool, dark place for up to 1 year. Once opened, store refrigerated and use within 2 weeks.

TIP: If using a pectin product with separate pectin and calcium packets, follow the package directions to mix calcium water. Use 5 teaspoons pectin powder and 2 tablespoons calcium water. Follow package directions for preparing recipe.

Per serving: calories 40 (calories from fat 0), protein 0g, fat 0g (saturated fat 0g), carbohydrates 11g, fiber 0g, cholesterol 0mg, sodium 0mg, sugar 10g
Dietary exchanges: ½ starch

Apple Pie Oatmeal

Prep Time:
10 minutes

Total Time:
10 minutes

**Makes
1 serving**

1 cup water
½ cup old-fashioned oats
1 dash salt (optional)

Apple Pie Topping:
2 teaspoons SPLENDA® Brown Sugar Blend
1 tablespoon chopped apple
1 dash apple pie spice

1. Bring water to a boil in a small saucepan. Stir in oats and salt. Cook, stirring occasionally, over medium heat 5 minutes.

or

Microwave Directions: Combine water, oats, and salt in a microwave-safe bowl. Cover tightly with heavy-duty plastic wrap; fold back a small edge to allow steam to escape. Microwave on HIGH 2½–3 minutes; stir well.

2. Top oatmeal with SPLENDA® Brown Sugar Blend, chopped apple, and spice.

Per serving: calories 200 (calories from fat 25), protein 7g, fat 3g (saturated fat 0g), carbohydrates 37g, fiber 5g, cholesterol 0mg, sodium 400mg, sugar 10g
Dietary exchanges: 2½ starches, ½ fat

Blueberry Corn Muffins

Prep Time:
10 minutes

Cook Time:
25 minutes

Total Time:
35 minutes

Makes
10 servings

1¾ cups all-purpose flour

½ cup yellow cornmeal

1¼ teaspoons baking powder

½ teaspoon baking soda

½ teaspoon salt

¾ cup **SPLENDA®** No Calorie Sweetener, Granulated

½ cup unsalted butter, softened

⅓ cup egg substitute

2 teaspoons vanilla

1 cup buttermilk

1 cup blueberries (frozen or fresh)

1. Preheat oven to 350°F. Spray a muffin pan with nonstick cooking spray or line muffin cups with paper liners. Set aside.

2. Blend dry ingredients together in a medium mixing bowl. Set aside.

3. Blend butter in a large mixing bowl until light and fluffy. Add egg substitute slowly. Scrape sides and continue to mix until butter forms small lumps. Add vanilla and buttermilk. Mix well. Add dry ingredients in three batches. Mix well and scrape the sides of the bowl after each addition.

4. Fold blueberries gently into batter. Scoop batter into prepared muffin cups, filling cups to the top. Bake in preheated oven 20–25 minutes or until done.

Per serving: calories 210 (calories from fat 90), protein 5g, fat 10g (saturated fat 6g), carbohydrates 26g, fiber 1g, cholesterol 25mg, sodium 280mg, sugar 2g
Dietary exchanges: 1½ starches, 2 fats

Fresh-Picked Strawberry Jam

3 pints ripe
   strawberries, stems
   removed

¾ cup water

1 (1.75 ounce)
   package fruit pectin
   for lower sugar
   recipes

¼ cup SPLENDA® Sugar
   Blend

Prep Time:
45 minutes

Cook Time:
8 minutes

Total Time:
53 minutes

**Makes
48 servings**

1. Wash jars and lids in hot soapy water; rinse with warm water. Fill boiling-water canner half full with water; add jars and water to cover. Bring water to a boil, reduce heat and simmer. Place lids in water to cover in a small saucepan; bring water to a simmer. Simmer until ready to use. Remove and drain jars and lids, one at a time, as needed for filling.

2. Cut strawberries in half; crush using potato masher or food processor. Place exactly 3 cups of crushed strawberries in a large saucepan; stir in water. Gradually add pectin, stirring until blended.

3. Bring mixture to a full rolling boil (a boil that doesn't stop bubbling when stirred) over medium-high heat. Boil for 1 minute, stirring constantly. Remove from heat; add SPLENDA® Sugar Blend, stirring until it dissolves. Skim off any foam with metal spoon. Allow to stand for 5 minutes to minimize separation of fruit and liquid.

4. Ladle hot jam into prepared jars, filling to within ¼ inch of tops. Wipe jar rims and threads. Cover with 2-piece lids. Screw bands tightly. Place jars on rack in canner. (Water must cover jars by 1–2 inches. Add boiling water, if necessary.) Cover; bring water to gentle boil.

5. Process 10 minutes. Remove jars and place upright on towel to cool completely. After jars cool, check seals by pressing center of lid with finger. (If lid springs back, lid is not sealed and refrigeration is necessary.) Store in a cool, dark place for up to 1 year. Once opened, store refrigerated and use within 2 weeks.

Per serving: calories 15 (calories from fat 0), protein 0g, fat 0g (saturated fat 0g), carbohydrates 4g, fiber 1g, cholesterol 0mg, sodium 0mg, sugar 1g
Dietary exchanges: free

Apricots and Ricotta Cheese Toast

Prep Time:
10 minutes

Cook Time:
18 minutes

Total Time:
28 minutes

**Makes
4 servings**

1 **cup water**

½ **cup SPLENDA®
Sugar Blend**

1 **vanilla bean, split
lengthwise**

1 **lemon, zested**

6 **fresh apricots,
peeled, halved and
pitted**

1 **tablespoon butter,
softened**

4 **slices bread, toasted**

1 **cup part-skim ricotta
cheese**

Optional Garnish:

Vanilla beans

1. Preheat broiler.

2. Combine water, SPLENDA® Sugar Blend, vanilla bean, and lemon zest in a non-aluminum saucepan. Bring to a boil over medium heat, stirring until SPLENDA® Sugar Blend dissolves; reduce heat and simmer 10 minutes or until mixture is reduced. Add apricots and simmer for 3–5 minutes or until apricots are just tender. Using a slotted spoon, remove apricots from syrup. Set aside.

3. Spread butter on bread slices. Broil until bread is lightly toasted.

4. Spoon ricotta cheese on each bread slice, Top with apricots and remaining syrup. Broil 2–3 minutes or until thoroughly heated and apricots begin to caramelize. Garnish with a vanilla bean, if desired. Serve immediately.

Per serving: calories 340 (calories from fat 80), protein 10g, fat 9g (saturated fat 5g), carbohydrates 49g, fiber 2g, cholesterol 25mg, sodium 240mg, sugar 34g
Dietary exchanges: 3 starches, 2 fats

Cinnamon Swirl Coffeecake

Prep Time:
20 minutes

Cook Time:
1 hour

Total Time:
1 hour,
20 minutes

**Makes
16 servings**

Cake Batter:

- **3 cups cake flour**
- **1 tablespoon baking powder**
- **¾ teaspoon baking soda**
- **½ cup butter**
- **1⅓ cups SPLENDA® No Calorie Sweetener, Granulated**
- **1 egg**
- **¼ cup egg substitute**
- **2 teaspoons vanilla extract**
- **½ cup unsweetened applesauce**
- **1½ cups light sour cream, divided**

Filling:

- **3 tablespoons brown sugar**
- **1 teaspoon ground cinnamon**

1. Preheat oven to 350°F. Spray a nonstick bundt pan with nonstick cooking spray. Set aside.

2. Sift cake flour, baking powder, and baking soda into a medium-sized mixing bowl; set aside. In a large mixing bowl, cream the butter with an electric mixer. Add SPLENDA® Granulated Sweetener and egg. Beat until smooth. Add the egg substitute and vanilla. Beat briefly to incorporate. Add applesauce and half of the sour cream. Beat until smooth. Add the sifted flour mixture and beat at medium speed just until smooth. Add remaining sour cream and blend just until incorporated and batter is uniform. Set aside.

3. Make Filling: Place ¼ of cake batter in a small bowl. Add brown sugar and cinnamon. Stir well.

4. Place ½ of the remaining cake batter into prepared pan. Top with filling. Swirl with knife. Top with remaining batter.

5. Bake 50–60 minutes or until a toothpick inserted near the center comes out clean.

Per serving: calories 200 (calories from fat 80), protein 4g, fat 9g (saturated fat 5g), carbohydrates 25g, fiber 1g, cholesterol 40mg, sodium 180mg, sugar 4g
Dietary exchanges: 1½ starches, 2 fats

Apricot Ginger Preserves

Prep Time:
1 hour,
30 minutes

Cook Time:
8 minutes

Total Time:
1 hour,
38 minutes

**Makes
96 servings**

4 quarts water
½ cup lemon juice
4½ pounds ripe apricots
¼ cup lemon juice
**2 teaspoons grated
fresh ginger**

**1 (1.75-ounce)
package low
methoxyl pectin
with calcium**
**1½ cups SPLENDA® No
Calorie Sweetener,
Granulated**

TIP: If using
a pectin
product with
separate
pectin and
calcium
packets,
follow the
package
directions to
mix calcium
water. Use
5 teaspoons
pectin
powder
and 2
tablespoons
calcium
water. Follow
package
directions for
preparing
recipe.

1. Wash jars and lids in hot soapy water; rinse with warm water. Fill boiling-water canner half full with water; add jars and water to cover. Bring water to a boil, reduce heat and simmer. Place lids in water to cover in a small saucepan; bring water to a simmer. Simmer until ready to use. Remove and drain jars and lids, one at a time, as needed for filling.

2. Combine 4 quarts water and ½ cup lemon juice in a large bowl; set aside. Fill a Dutch oven ¾ full with water; bring to a boil. Immerse apricots for 20 seconds or until skins easily peel away; remove with slotted spoon and plunge into ice water. Slip skin off apricots using a paring knife. Cut apricots in half; remove pits. Place in the lemon juice and water solution to prevent browning; drain. Place the apricots in food processor in batches; process until finely chopped. Measure exactly 6 cups of fruit.

3. Combine chopped apricots, ¼ cup lemon juice, ginger, and pectin in a large Dutch oven; stirring until pectin dissolves. Let stand 10 minutes.

4. Bring mixture to a full rolling boil (a boil that doesn't stop bubbling when stirred) over medium-high heat. Boil 1 minute, stirring constantly. Remove from heat; add SPLENDA® Granulated Sweetener, stirring until SPLENDA® Granulated Sweetener dissolves. Skim off any foam with metal spoon.

5. Ladle hot preserves immediately into prepared jars, filling to within ¼ inch of tops. Wipe jar rims and threads. Cover with 2-piece lids. Screw bands tightly. Place jars on rack in canner. (Water must cover jars by 1–2 inches. Add boiling water, if necessary.) Cover; bring water to gentle boil.

6. Process 10 minutes. Remove jars and place upright on towel to cool completely. After jars cool, check seals by pressing center of lid with finger. (If lid springs back, lid is not sealed and refrigeration is necessary.) Store in a cool, dark place for up to 1 year. Once opened, store refrigerated and use within 2 weeks.

Per serving: calories 10 (calories from fat 0) protein 0g, fat 0g (saturated fat 0g), carbohydrates 3g, fiber 1g, cholesterol 0mg, sodium 0mg, sugar 2g
Dietary exchanges: free

Meal Starters and Salads

Raspberry Cocktail Sauce with Chilled Shrimp

Prep Time: 5 minutes
Total Time: 2 hours, 5 minutes

Makes 32 servings

Cocktail Sauce:

- 1 cup no-sugar-added raspberry preserves
- ¼ cup prepared horseradish
- 3 tablespoons SPLENDA® No Calorie Sweetener, Granulated
- 2 tablespoons tomato paste
- 3 teaspoons sherry wine vinegar
- 2 tablespoons Worcestershire sauce
- 1 clove garlic, minced
- 1 jalapeño pepper, minced
- ½ teaspoon salt
- 1 pinch black pepper
- 2 pounds cooked, peeled and deveined shrimp

1. Place cocktail sauce ingredients in a food processor or a blender. Process or blend for 30 seconds or until smooth.

2. Chill cocktail sauce at least 2 hours before serving. Serve with shrimp. Cocktail sauce will keep, refrigerated, for 5 days.

Per serving: calories 45 (calories from fat 0), protein 6g, fat 0g (saturated fat 0g), carbohydrates 4g, fiber 1g, cholesterol 55mg, sodium 125mg, sugar 3g
Dietary exchanges: *1 lean meat*

Orange-Almond Salad

Prep Time:
15 minutes
Total Time:
15 minutes

**Makes
4 servings**

3 cups assorted greens

2 navel oranges, peeled and separated into sections

½ cup thinly sliced celery

2 tablespoons chopped green onion

Dressing:

¼ cup cider vinegar

¼ cup SPLENDA® No Calorie Sweetener, Granulated

2 teaspoons vegetable oil

¼ cup toasted slivered almonds

1. Combine greens, orange sections, celery, and green onion in a large mixing bowl. Set aside.

2. Combine vinegar, SPLENDA® Granulated Sweetener, and vegetable oil in a small mixing bowl. Stir with a whisk until well blended. Drizzle dressing mixture evenly over greens mixture. Toss gently to coat.

3. To serve, place 1 cup salad mixture on a serving plate and garnish by sprinkling 1 tablespoon almonds over the top of the salad. Serve immediately.

Per serving: calories 120 (calories from fat 60), protein 3g, fat 7g (saturated fat 1g), carbohydrates 14g, fiber 4g, cholesterol 0mg, sodium 25mg, sugar 10g
Dietary exchanges: ½ fruit, 1 vegetable, 1½ fats

Raw Broccoli Salad

Prep Time:
10 minutes

Total Time:
10 minutes

**Makes
6 servings**

4 cups broccoli florets
or broccolini

¼ cup red onion,
minced

2 tablespoons
SPLENDA® No
Calorie Sweetener,
Granulated

2 tablespoons cider
vinegar

2 tablespoons light
mayonnaise

2 tablespoons
sunflower seeds,
roasted and salted

3 tablespoons seedless
raisins

1. Discard broccoli stems and finely chop florets or broccolini. Set aside.

2. Place remaining ingredients in a medium mixing bowl. Mix well. Add broccoli florets or broccolini. Toss until coated. Chill until ready to serve.

Per serving: calories 60 (calories from fat 15), protein 3g, fat 2g (saturated fat 0g), carbohydrates 10g, fiber 2g, cholesterol 0mg, sodium 85mg, sugar 6g
Dietary exchanges: 1 vegetable, ½ fat

Citrus Salsa

4 **Roma tomatoes**

2 **large oranges,
peeled and diced**

1 **large Vidalia onion,
peeled and chopped**

2 **jalapeño peppers,
seeded and minced**

2 **tablespoons fresh
lime juice**

¼ **cup fresh orange
juice**

3 **(1-gram) packets
SPLENDA® No Calorie
Sweetener**

1 **tablespoon chopped
fresh cilantro**

1 **teaspoon salt**

Prep Time:
15 minutes

Total Time:
1 hour,
15 minutes

**Makes
5 servings**

1. Bring small saucepan of water to a boil. Blanch tomatoes for 30 seconds, and then rinse with cold water. Peel and chop tomatoes.

2. Place all ingredients in a large bowl and stir until mixed thoroughly. Allow to stand at room temperature for one hour. Mix and serve. Refrigerate any unused salsa.

Per serving: calories 70 (calories from fat 0), protein 2g, fat 0g (saturated fat 0g), carbohydrates 16g, fiber 3g, cholesterol 0mg, sodium 470mg, sugar 12g

Dietary exchanges: ½ fruit, 1½ vegetables

Sweet Red Pepper Hummus

Prep Time:
10 minutes

Cook Time:
5 minutes

Total Time:
15 minutes

**Makes
15 servings**

Olive oil-flavored
  cooking spray
2 cups chopped red
  bell pepper
1 tablespoon extra
  virgin olive oil
2 tablespoons fresh
  lemon juice
½ teaspoon apple cider
  vinegar

2 tablespoons
  chopped fresh
  parsley
½ teaspoon salt
½ teaspoon cumin
2 tablespoons
  SPLENDA® No
  Calorie Sweetener,
  Granulated
1 (19-ounce) can
  garbanzo beans,
  drained

Spray nonstick sauté pan with nonstick olive oil cooking
spray. Sauté red peppers for 4–5 minutes. Set aside.
In food processor, add all ingredients including red
peppers. Purée for 1 minute, scrape the sides, and
continue to purée until smooth. Refrigerate until serving
time.

Per serving: calories 60 (calories from fat 15), protein 2g, fat 1g
(saturated fat 0g), carbohydrates 10g, fiber 2g, cholesterol 0mg,
sodium 190mg, sugar 2g
Dietary exchanges: ½ starch

Ginger Noodle Salad

Prep Time:
20 minutes

Total Time:
20 minutes

**Makes
4 servings**

**4 ounces dry spaghetti
or capellini**

Dressing:

**1 tablespoon minced
ginger**

**3 tablespoons
SPLENDA® No
Calorie Sweetener,
Granulated**

1 tablespoon ketchup

¼ cup lite soy sauce

**¼ teaspoon Chinese
chile paste (add
more if you want it
spicier)**

1 tablespoon water

**2 tablespoons fresh
lime juice**

**1 teaspoon sesame oil
or vegetable oil**

**2 cups mixed salad
greens**

1. Cook pasta following package directions.

2. Place ginger, SPLENDA® Granulated Sweetener,
ketchup, soy sauce, chile paste, and water in a
medium saucepan. Simmer on medium-low heat
1 minute. Remove from heat. Add lime juice and
sesame oil. Mix well. Add noodles and stir well. Serve
immediately for a warm salad. Chill 15–20 minutes for
a cold salad.

3. To serve: place noodles on top of greens. Garnish,
if desired.

*Per serving: calories 130 (calories from fat 15), protein 5g, fat 2g
(saturated fat 0g), carbohydrates 24g, fiber 2g, cholesterol 0mg,
sodium 590mg, sugar 1g*
Dietary exchanges: 1½ starches

Cucumber and Onion Salad

2½ cups thinly sliced unpeeled cucumbers

½ cup thinly sliced onions

⅓ cup SPLENDA® No Calorie Sweetener, Granulated

⅓ cup white vinegar

¼ teaspoon salt

⅛ teaspoon black pepper

Prep Time:
15 minutes

Total Time:
2 hours,
15 minutes

**Makes
6 servings**

1. Place cucumbers and onions in a non-metallic medium bowl.

2. Combine remaining ingredients in a small mixing bowl. Stir well. Pour over cucumbers and onions. Cover and refrigerate for at least 2 hours. Stir occasionally.

Per serving: calories 15 (calories from fat 0), protein 1g, fat 0g (saturated fat 0g), carbohydrates 3g, fiber 1g, cholesterol 0mg, sodium 100mg, sugar 2g
Dietary exchanges: free

Sweet and Spicy BLT

Prep Time:
10 minutes

Total Time:
10 minutes

**Makes
5 servings**

Seasoning Mix:

- **1 tablespoon SPLENDA® No Calorie Sweetener, Granulated**
- **¼ teaspoon cayenne**
- **¼ teaspoon garlic powder**
- **1 teaspoon paprika**

- **10 slices extra lean turkey bacon**
- **10 slices wheat bread**
- **5 tablespoons fat-free ranch dressing**
- **5 leaves green lettuce**
- **10 slices fresh tomato**

1. Place ingredients for seasoning mix in a small bowl. Mix well.

2. Place bacon on a microwaveable plate. Top each slice with ½ teaspoon seasoning mix. Microwave bacon following label instructions.

3. Toast bread. Spread ranch dressing on toast. Assemble sandwiches with cooked bacon, lettuce, and tomato.

Per serving: calories 220 (calories from fat 60), protein 9g, fat 6g (saturated fat 2g), carbohydrates 35g, fiber 5g, cholesterol 15mg, sodium 720mg, sugar 5g
Dietary exchanges: *2 starches, 1 medium-fat meat*

Baby Spinach 'n Bacon Salad

Prep Time:
15 minutes

Total Time:
15 minutes

**Makes
4 servings**

1 **(7-ounce) bag baby spinach greens***

½ **cup fat-free salad croutons**

Dressing:

¼ **cup white vinegar**

¼ **cup water**

¼ **cup Dijon mustard**

3 **tablespoons SPLENDA® No Calorie Sweetener, Granulated**

5 **slices turkey bacon**

¼ **cup chopped red onion**

2 **garlic cloves, minced**

Regular spinach may be used in place of baby spinach but will result in a less delicate salad.

1. Place spinach greens in a large mixing bowl. Remove any undesirable leaves or large stems. Add croutons. Set aside.

2. Make Dressing. Blend together vinegar, water, mustard, and SPLENDA® Granulated Sweetener in a small mixing bowl. Set aside.

3. Finely slice bacon into small strips. Place in a medium saucepan and fry over medium-high heat until crispy (approximately 3–4 minutes).

4. Add onion and garlic and cook over medium-high heat 1–2 minutes.

5. Add vinegar mixture and simmer 1–2 minutes. Pour over spinach and croutons. Toss well. Serve immediately.

Per serving: *calories 80 (calories from fat 35), protein 5g, fat 4g (saturated fat 1g), carbohydrates 8g, fiber 2g, cholesterol 10mg, sodium 620mg, sugar 1g*
Dietary exchanges: *1 vegetable, 1 fat*

Sweet and Crunchy Deli-Style Pickles

- **7 pickling cucumbers, quartered**
- **1 cup water**
- **½ cup rice vinegar**
- **⅓ cup SPLENDA® No Calorie Sweetener, Granulated**
- **1 tablespoon kosher salt**
- **1 whole clove**
- **1 teaspoon mustard seed**
- **1 teaspoon whole black peppercorns**
- **1 teaspoon peeled, chopped fresh ginger**
- **½ jalapeño pepper, seeded and chopped**
- **2 garlic cloves**

Prep Time:
15 minutes
Total Time:
4 days,
15 minutes

Makes
24 servings

1. Place quartered pickles in a clean 1-quart canning jar. Set aside.

2. Combine remaining ingredients in a small saucepan. Simmer over low heat until salt dissolves.

3. Pour hot pickling juice over pickles to fill jar. Cover tightly with lid and refrigerate 4–5 days before serving. Pickle flavor and sweetness intensity increase over time.

Per serving: calories 10 (calories from fat 0), protein 0g, fat 0g (saturated fat 0g), carbohydrates 2g, fiber 1g, cholesterol 0mg, sodium 240mg, sugar 1g
Dietary exchanges: free

Sweet and Crunchy Nuts

Prep Time:
5 minutes

Cook Time:
30 minutes

Total Time:
35 minutes

**Makes
8 servings**

¾ **cup pecan halves**

¾ **cup walnut halves**

½ **cup whole blanched almonds**

1 **egg white, lightly beaten**

⅓ **cup SPLENDA® No Calorie Sweetener, Granulated**

½ **teaspoon ground cinnamon**

1. Preheat oven to 300°F. Spray a 15×10×1-inch pan with nonstick cooking spray.

2. Combine pecans, walnuts, and almonds in a mixing bowl; add egg white, tossing to coat.

3. Combine SPLENDA® Granulated Sweetener and cinnamon; sprinkle over nuts, tossing to coat. Spread mixture evenly in prepared pan.

4. Bake 30 minutes or until nuts are toasted, stirring every 10 minutes. Cool on waxed paper. Store in an airtight tin.

Per serving: calories 210 (calories from fat 180), protein 5g, fat 20g (saturated fat 2g), carbohydrates 5g, fiber 3g, cholesterol 0mg, sodium 10mg, sugar 1g
Dietary exchanges: ½ starch, 4 fats

Berrilicious Salsa

- 1 cup fresh raspberries, cut into halves
- 1 cup fresh blackberries, cut into halves
- 1 medium apple, coarsely chopped
- 1 kiwi fruit, peeled and coarsely chopped
- 1 orange, peeled, seeded, and coarsely chopped
- 1 tablespoon chopped red onion

- 1 green onion, thinly sliced
- 1 tablespoon diced green chile peppers
- ¼ cup SPLENDA® No Calorie Sweetener, Granulated
- 1 tablespoon fresh lime juice
- 1 tablespoon white wine vinegar

Prep Time:
30 minutes
Total Time:
1 hour,
30 minutes

**Makes
12 servings**

Combine all ingredients; cover and chill 1 hour.

Per serving: calories 30 (calories from fat 0), protein 0g, fat 0g (saturated fat 0g), carbohydrates 7g, fiber 2g, cholesterol 0mg, sodium 10mg, sugar 5g
Dietary exchanges: ½ fruit

Entrées and Sides

Lemon Glazed Jumbo Shrimp Salad

Prep Time:
10 minutes

Cook Time:
12 minutes

Total Time:
22 minutes

**Makes
4 servings**

1 tablespoon extra-virgin olive oil

8 jumbo shrimp, peeled and deveined

½ cup fresh lemon juice

½ cup cider vinegar

½ cup SPLENDA® No Calorie Sweetener, Granulated

½ teaspoon crushed red pepper

1 jalapeño, trimmed, seeded and thinly sliced

2 cups baby arugula leaves

½ cup thinly sliced red bell pepper

½ cup thinly sliced mango

Salt and pepper to taste

1. Heat oil in a medium skillet over high heat; add shrimp and cook 1 minute. Stir in lemon juice and cook 3–4 minutes or until shrimp are cooked through. Using tongs, transfer shrimp to a plate. Add vinegar, SPLENDA® Granulated Sweetener, crushed red pepper, and jalapeño; bring to a boil and cook 4–5 minutes or until reduced by half, then remove from heat and set aside.

2. Place arugula, red pepper, and mango in a large bowl; toss gently with some of the dressing and season to taste.

3. Divide arugula mixture among 4 serving plates; top each salad with 2 shrimp and drizzle evenly with the warm vinegar mixture.

Per serving: calories 120 (calories from fat 40), protein 12g, fat 4g (saturated fat 1g), carbohydrates 10g, fiber 1g, cholesterol 105mg, sodium 220mg, sugar 6g
Dietary exchanges: ½ starch, 1 lean meat, 1 vegetable

Easy Lemon Chicken

Prep Time:
10 minutes

Cook Time:
10 minutes

Total Time:
20 minutes

**Makes
4 servings**

1 teaspoon cornstarch

1 tablespoon low-sodium soy sauce

12 ounces chicken breast tenders, cut in thirds

¼ cup fresh lemon juice

¼ cup low-sodium soy sauce

¼ cup fat-free chicken broth

1 teaspoon fresh ginger, minced

2 cloves garlic, minced

1 tablespoon SPLENDA® No Calorie Sweetener, Granulated

1 teaspoon cornstarch

1 tablespoon vegetable oil

¼ cup red bell pepper, sliced into 2-inch strips

¼ cup green bell pepper, sliced into 2-inch strips

1. Mix 1 teaspoon cornstarch and 1 tablespoon soy sauce in a small mixing bowl. Add sliced chicken tenders. Place in refrigerator and marinate for 10 minutes.

2. Stir the lemon juice, ¼ cup soy sauce, chicken broth, ginger, garlic, SPLENDA® Granulated Sweetener, and 1 teaspoon cornstarch together in a medium-sized mixing bowl.

3. Heat oil in a medium frying pan. Add chicken and cook over medium-high heat for 3–4 minutes or until just done. Add sauce and sliced peppers. Cook 1–2 minutes more or until sauce thickens and peppers are slightly tender.

Per serving: calories 150 (calories from fat 40), protein 21g, fat 5g (saturated fat 1g), carbohydrates 6g, fiber 1g, cholesterol 50mg, sodium 730mg, sugar 1g
Dietary exchanges: ½ starch, 3 lean meats

Chicken Cacciatore Over Pasta

Prep Time:
10 minutes

Cook Time:
23 minutes

Total Time:
33 minutes

**Makes
6 servings**

- 1 pound skinless, boneless chicken breast halves
- ½ cup chopped onion
- ½ cup chopped green bell pepper
- 1 (16-ounce) can chopped tomatoes, drained
- 1 (8-ounce) can tomato sauce
- 2 tablespoons SPLENDA® No Calorie Sweetener, Granulated
- 1½ teaspoons Italian seasoning
- ⅓ cup sliced ripe olives
- ⅛ teaspoon black pepper
- 3 cups hot cooked noodles (or any favorite pasta), rinsed and drained

1. Slice chicken breasts into 32 pieces.

2. Spray a large skillet with olive oil-flavored nonstick cooking spray. Sauté chicken, onion, and green pepper for 6–8 minutes. Stir in drained tomatoes and tomato sauce.

3. Add SPLENDA® Granulated Sweetener, Italian seasoning, olives, and black pepper. Mix well to combine. Lower heat and simmer for 10–15 minutes, stirring occasionally.

4. For each serving, place ½ cup pasta on a plate and spoon ⅔ cup sauce over top.

Per serving: calories 210 (calories from fat 40), protein 21g, fat 4g (saturated fat 1g), carbohydrates 22g, fiber 3g, cholesterol 65mg, sodium 460mg, sugar 5g
Dietary exchanges: 1 starch, 1 vegetable, 2 lean meats

Quick Glazed Pork Loin

Prep Time:
10 minutes

Cook Time:
30 minutes

Total Time:
40 minutes

**Makes
4 servings**

1 **pound pork
tenderloin**

¼ **cup water**

2 **tablespoons tomato
paste**

1 **tablespoon orange
juice concentrate**

2½ **teaspoons chili
powder**

⅛ **teaspoon salt**

1 **tablespoon
SPLENDA® No
Calorie Sweetener,
Granulated**

1 **teaspoon white
vinegar**

1 **(14-ounce) package
frozen vegetable
blend**

1. Preheat oven to 425°F. Rinse pork loin and pat dry.
Set aside.

2. Mix water, tomato paste, orange juice concentrate,
chili powder, salt, SPLENDA® Granulated Sweetener,
and white vinegar in a small mixing bowl.

3. Place pork loin in a 13×9-inch pan. Cover with half
of the glaze. Bake 15 minutes in preheated oven.

4. Remove pork loin from oven. Cover with remaining
glaze. Place vegetables around pork loin. Bake an
additional 15 minutes or until the vegetables are hot
and the pork loin is completely cooked.*

*Pork loin is completely cooked when poked with a fork in the thickest
section of the loin and juice runs clear or meat thermometer registers
155°F. Let roast stand for 10 minutes before slicing. This allows juices to
settle in the meat creating a juicier cut of meat.*

Per serving: calories 220 (calories from fat 60), protein 24g, fat 6g
(saturated fat 2g), carbohydrates 18g, fiber 5g, cholesterol 65mg,
sodium 240mg, sugar 2g
Dietary exchanges: 1 starch, 3 lean meats

Baked Salmon
with Orange-Ginger Sauce

Prep Time:
15 minutes

Cook Time:
15 minutes

Total Time:
30 minutes

**Makes
2 servings**

2½-inch piece fresh ginger root

1 cup fresh orange juice

¼ cup **SPLENDA®** No Calorie Sweetener, Granulated

2 tablespoons fat-free half and half

¼ teaspoon cornstarch

¼ teaspoon salt (optional)

2 tablespoons unsalted butter, softened

2 cups frozen stir-fry vegetable blend

2 (4-ounce) salmon fillets

1. Preheat oven to 450°F.

2. Make sauce. Peel ginger root and slice into 10 slices. Pour orange juice into a small saucepan. Add SPLENDA® Granulated Sweetener and ginger root. Bring to a rolling boil over medium high heat. Boil 10–12 minutes or until orange juice has reduced to approximately 2 tablespoons. Remove sauce from heat. Remove ginger slices using a fork and discard. Set sauce aside.

3. Mix together the half and half, cornstarch, and salt. Set aside. Whisk the softened butter, 1 tablespoon at a time, into the 2 tablespoons of orange juice. Stir until melted. Add half and half mixture. Stir well. Place saucepan back on heat. Heat over medium-high heat until boiling.

4. Remove sauce from heat and mix in a blender 15–20 seconds or until smooth and lighter in color. Set aside.

5. Prepare salmon. Place vegetables in an 8×8-inch baking pan. Place salmon fillets on top of the vegetables. Bake in preheated oven 10–15 minutes or until cooked through, but still tender.

6. Place vegetables and salmon on serving plates. Pour sauce over salmon. Serve immediately. Serve with steamed rice, if desired.

Per serving: calories 440 (calories from fat 180), protein 30g, fat 20g (saturated fat 8g), carbohydrates 38g, fiber 7g, cholesterol 95mg, sodium 440mg, sugar 14g
Dietary exchanges: 1 starch, 4 lean meats, 1 vegetable, 1 fruit, 2 fats

Stir-Fried Green Beans

Prep Time:
10 minutes

Cook Time:
10 minutes

Total Time:
20 minutes

**Makes
6 servings**

Stir-Fry Sauce:

1½ tablespoons minced garlic

1½ tablespoons minced fresh ginger

2 scallions (white and green parts), minced

2 tablespoons dry sherry*

2 tablespoons SPLENDA® No Calorie Sweetener, Granulated

2 tablespoons soy sauce

1 tablespoon water

Stir-Fry:

2 tablespoons peanut or vegetable oil

1½ pounds green beans, trimmed and rinsed

2 tablespoons water

For dietary purposes, please note that this recipe contains alcohol.

1. Make Stir-Fry Sauce. Combine the Stir-Fry Sauce ingredients in a small bowl. Set aside.

2. Make Stir-Fry. In a large skillet or wok, heat the oil and stir-fry the green beans until they are barely crisp (approximately 2 minutes).

3. Add the water and continue stir-frying for another 2 minutes, until the beans are slightly tender and water has evaporated.

4. Add the sauce and continue stir-frying for 5–6 minutes, until the beans are tender but not overcooked. Serve immediately.

Per serving: calories 90 (calories from fat 40), protein 3g, fat 5g (saturated fat 1g), carbohydrates 10g, fiber 4g, cholesterol 0mg, sodium 310mg, sugar 3g
Dietary exchanges: 1½ vegetables, 1 fat

Boston-Style Baked Beans

Prep Time:
15 minutes

Cook Time:
45 minutes

Total Time:
1 hour

**Makes
18 servings**

4 **(15-ounce) cans
navy beans**

½ **pound bacon,
chopped**

1 **medium onion,
chopped**

¼ **cup yellow mustard**

⅓ **cup SPLENDA® No
Calorie Sweetener,
Granulated**

2 **tablespoons robust
molasses**

1. Preheat oven to 350°F.

2. Drain navy beans and reserve 1¼ cups liquid.

3. Fry bacon in a large skillet until browned. Remove bacon and reserve half of the bacon fat.

4. Fry onion in reserved bacon fat and cook until translucent. Stir in beans and remaining ingredients.

5. Pour beans into a 3-quart baking dish. Bake in preheated oven 45 minutes.

Per serving: calories 140 (calories from fat 25), protein 9g, fat 3g (saturated fat 1g), carbohydrates 21g, fiber 5g, cholesterol 5mg, sodium 520mg, sugar 3g
Dietary exchanges: 1½ starches, 1 lean meat

Asparagus with Sesame-Ginger Sauce

Prep Time:
10 minutes

Cook Time:
10 minutes

Total Time:
20 minutes

**Makes
7 servings**

1 tablespoon soy sauce

1 tablespoon rice vinegar

1 tablespoon peanut oil

1 tablespoon water

1 tablespoon tahini (puréed sesame seeds)

1 teaspoon chopped fresh ginger

½ teaspoon chopped garlic

1 tablespoon SPLENDA® No Calorie Sweetener, Granulated

1 pinch red pepper flakes

48 medium-size asparagus spears, trimmed, peeled and cleaned

1. In a food processor or blender, combine everything except the asparagus and mix until thoroughly blended. Set aside.

2. Half-fill a large skillet with water, cover and bring to a boil. Add the asparagus and simmer just until crisp-tender (approximately 4–5 minutes). Drain well but do not rinse.

3. Transfer to serving bowl. Pour the sauce over the hot asparagus and toss to coat. Serve warm or at room temperature.

Per serving: calories 60 (calories from fat 30), protein 3g, fat 3g (saturated fat 1g), carbohydrates 6g, fiber 3g, cholesterol 0mg, sodium 135mg, sugar 2g
Dietary exchanges: *1 vegetable, ½ fat*

Corn Relish

1¼ cups white vinegar

1¼ cups water

¼ cup **SPLENDA® No Calorie Sweetener, Granulated**

1½ teaspoons dry mustard

1¼ teaspoons celery seeds

1 teaspoon ground turmeric

1 teaspoon salt

3 cups fresh or frozen corn kernels

¼ cup chopped onion

⅓ cup chopped green bell pepper

⅓ cup chopped red bell pepper

Prep Time:
45 minutes

Cook Time:
15 minutes

Total Time:
1 hour

**Makes
32 servings**

1. Wash jars and lids in hot soapy water; rinse with warm water. Fill boiling-water canner half full with water; add jars and water to cover. Bring water to a boil, reduce heat and simmer. Place lids in water to cover in a small saucepan; bring to a simmer. Simmer until ready to use. Remove and drain jars and lids, one at a time, as needed for filling.

2. Combine vinegar, water, SPLENDA® Granulated Sweetener, mustard, celery seeds, turmeric, and salt in a large Dutch oven, stirring until SPLENDA® Granulated Sweetener dissolves. Add corn, onion, and bell peppers and bring to a boil; reduce heat and simmer, covered, for 15 minutes.

3. Pack hot vegetables immediately into prepared jars using a slotted spoon, filling to within ¼-inch from top. Ladle liquid into jars, filling to within ¼-inch from top. Wipe rims and threads. Cover with 2-piece lids. Screw bands tightly. Place jars on rack in canner. (Water must cover jars by 1–2 inches. Add boiling water, if necessary.) Cover; bring water to a gentle boil.

4. Process 15 minutes. Remove jars and place upright on towel to cool completely. After jars cool, check seals by pressing center of lid with finger. (If lid springs back, lid is not sealed and refrigeration is necessary.) Store in a cool, dark place for up to 1 year. Once opened, store refrigerated and use within 2 weeks.

Per serving: calories 15 (calories from fat 0), protein 1g, fat 0g (saturated fat 0g), carbohydrates 4g, fiber 0g, cholesterol 0mg, sodium 75mg, sugar 0g
Dietary exchanges: free

Citrus Glazed Chicken with Almonds

Prep Time:
20 minutes

Cook Time:
30 minutes

Total Time:
50 minutes

**Makes
4 servings**

4 **(4-ounce) boneless, skinless chicken breasts**

3 **tablespoons orange juice concentrate, thawed**

2 **tablespoons fresh lemon juice**

½ **cup chicken broth**

3 **tablespoons SPLENDA® No Calorie Sweetener, Granulated**

1½ **teaspoons cornstarch**

1 **tablespoon unsalted butter**

1 **tablespoon chopped fresh chives**

1 **tablespoon chopped fresh parsley**

¼ **cup almond slices, toasted**

1. Preheat oven to 425°F. Place chicken breasts on an ungreased baking sheet. Brush with 1 tablespoon of orange juice concentrate (reserve remaining concentrate for sauce). Bake in oven 15–20 minutes or until cooked through.

2. Place remaining orange juice concentrate, lemon juice, and chicken broth in a small saucepan. Blend together SPLENDA® Granulated Sweetener and cornstarch in a small bowl. Stir cornstarch mixture into broth. Heat over medium-high heat and simmer 8–10 minutes or until the sauce starts to thicken slightly. Remove from heat. Whisk butter into sauce. Add chives and parsley. Pour sauce over chicken breasts. Sprinkle almonds over breasts and serve.

Per serving: calories 220 (calories from fat 70), protein 28g, fat 8g (saturated fat 2g), carbohydrates 8g, fiber 1g, cholesterol 75mg, sodium 200mg, sugar 6g
Dietary exchanges: ½ starch, 4 lean meats

Chili Vegetarian Style

Prep Time:
20 minutes

Cook Time:
28 minutes

Total Time:
48 minutes

**Makes
16 servings**

- 1 tablespoon extra virgin olive oil
- 1 jalapeño pepper, seeded and finely chopped
- ½ cup chopped onion
- 1⅓ cups chopped red and yellow bell peppers
- 6 teaspoons chili powder
- 1½ teaspoons paprika
- ¼ teaspoon garlic powder
- ¾ teaspoon ground cayenne pepper
- ½ cup SPLENDA® No Calorie Sweetener, Granulated

- 3 tablespoons balsamic vinegar
- 1 (28-ounce) can crushed tomatoes with thick tomato purée
- 1 (19-ounce) can black beans, undrained
- 2 (19-ounce) cans dark red kidney beans, undrained
- 1 (19-ounce) can cannellini beans, undrained
- 1 (10-ounce) package frozen whole kernel corn

1. In a large, nonstick stockpot heat olive oil. Sauté jalapeño pepper, onion, and red and yellow peppers over medium heat until onions are translucent (5–8 minutes).

2. Add the remaining ingredients and slowly bring to a boil. Cover pot and simmer on low heat for 20 minutes. Serve hot. Chili tastes best when allowed to sit overnight. Refrigerate chili in covered pot overnight. Bring to a boil over a low heat, stirring constantly.

Per serving: calories 160 (calories from fat 15), protein 9g, fat 2g (saturated fat 0g), carbohydrates 30g, fiber 10g, cholesterol 0mg, sodium 500mg, sugar 3g
Dietary exchanges: 1½ starches, 1 vegetable

Cranberry Apple Relish

1 (12-ounce) bag fresh
  cranberries

1 cup SPLENDA® No
  Calorie Sweetener,
  Granulated

1 cup water

3 tablespoons orange
  juice concentrate

1 medium apple,
  peeled, cored, and
  diced

⅓ cup golden raisins

Prep Time:
20 minutes

Total Time:
3 hours,
20 minutes

**Makes
20 servings**

1. Place cranberries, SPLENDA® Granulated Sweetener, water, and orange juice concentrate in a medium saucepan. Bring to a boil and boil 3–4 minutes or until cranberries start to thicken and water has reduced by about half.

2. Remove from pan and place in medium bowl. Cover and refrigerate 2–3 hours or overnight.

3. Add diced apple and half of the raisins to cranberries. Stir well. Refrigerate until ready to serve. Just before serving, sprinkle remaining raisins over cranberries as a garnish. Serve chilled as an accompaniment to roast meats or poultry.

Per serving: calories 25 (calories from fat 0), protein 0g, fat 0g (saturated fat 0g), carbohydrates 6g, fiber 1g, cholesterol 0mg, sodium 0mg, sugar 4g
Dietary exchanges: ½ starch

Kid Pleasers

KOOL-AID® INVISIBLE® Kool Pops

Prep Time:
5 minutes

Total Time:
3 hours,
5 minutes

**Makes
16 servings**

1 (.23-ounce) envelope KOOL-AID® INVISIBLE® Watermelon Kiwi Flavor Unsweetened Soft Drink Mix

1 cup SPLENDA® No Calorie Sweetener, Granulated

Water

16 (5-ounce) paper or plastic cups

16 ice cream sticks

1. Empty contents of envelope into large pitcher. Add SPLENDA® Granulated Sweetener. Add cold water to equal 2 quarts. Stir to dissolve.

2. Pour soft drink evenly into paper cups. Freeze 1½ hours or until almost firm. Insert ice cream stick into center of each cup.

3. Freeze an additional 1½ hours or until firm. Store in freezer.

Per serving: calories 2 (calories from fat 0), protein 0g, fat 0g (saturated fat 0g), carbohydrates 0g, fiber 0g, cholesterol 0mg, sodium 15mg, sugar 0g
Dietary exchanges: free

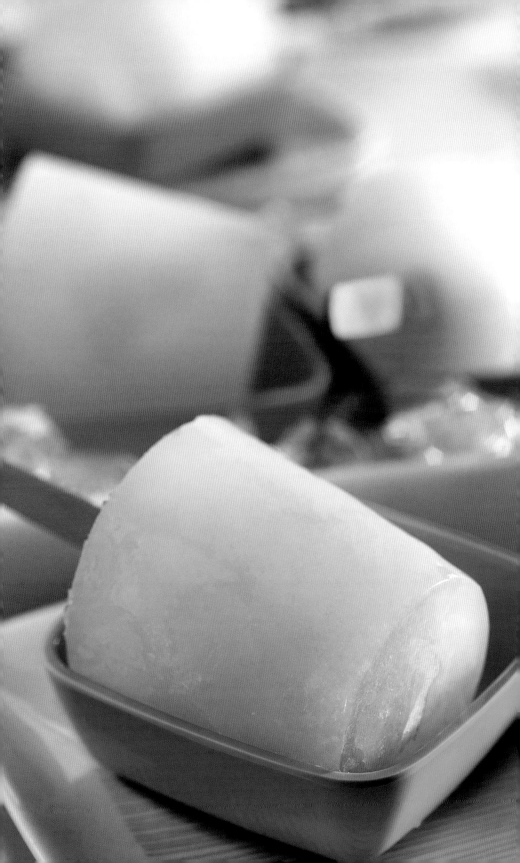

Peanut Butter Cookie Bites

Prep Time:
20 minutes

Cook Time:
9 minutes

Total Time:
29 minutes

**Makes
24 servings**

¼ cup margarine, softened

1 cup creamy style peanut butter

¼ cup egg substitute

2 tablespoons honey

½ teaspoon vanilla

1 cup SPLENDA® No Calorie Sweetener, Granulated

1½ cups all-purpose flour

½ teaspoon baking soda

½ teaspoon salt

1. Preheat oven to 350°F.

2. Beat margarine and peanut butter in a large mixing bowl with an electric mixer until creamy, approximately 1 minute.

3. Add egg substitute, honey, and vanilla. Beat on high speed for approximately 1½ minutes.

4. Add SPLENDA® Granulated Sweetener and beat on medium speed until well blended, approximately 30 seconds.

5. Combine flour, baking soda, and salt in a small mixing bowl. Slowly add flour mixture to peanut butter mixture, beating on low speed until well-blended, about 1½ minutes. Mixture may be crumbly.

6. Roll level tablespoons of dough into balls and drop onto a lightly oiled or parchment-lined sheet pan, 2 inches apart. Flatten each ball with a fork, pressing a crisscross pattern into each cookie. Bake 7–9 minutes or until light brown around the edges. Cool on wire rack.

Per serving: calories 120 (calories from fat 70), protein 4g, fat 8g (saturated fat 1g), carbohydrates 10g, fiber 1g, cholesterol 0mg, sodium 150mg, sugar 2g
Dietary exchanges: ½ starch, 1½ fats

S'Mores Campfire Pie

Prep Time:
15 minutes

Cook Time:
2 hours

Total Time:
10 hours,
15 minutes

**Makes
8 servings**

Filling:

- ½ cup **SPLENDA®** Sugar Blend
- ⅓ cup fat-free half and half
- 1 teaspoon vanilla extract
- 4 (1-ounce) squares unsweetened chocolate, chopped
- 1 (9-inch) graham cracker crust

Meringue:

- 4 egg whites
- ¼ teaspoon cream of tartar
- 1 teaspoon vanilla extract
- ½ cup **SPLENDA®** Sugar Blend

1. Prepare Filling: Combine SPLENDA® Sugar Blend and half and half in a small saucepan. Cook over medium heat, stirring constantly, until SPLENDA® Sugar Blend dissolves. Stir in vanilla; add chocolate, stirring until chocolate melts. Pour mixture into crust. Set aside.

2. Prepare Meringue: Preheat oven to 225°F.

3. Combine egg whites, cream of tartar, and vanilla in a large mixing bowl; beat at high speed with an electric mixer until foamy. Gradually add SPLENDA® Sugar Blend, 1 tablespoon at a time, beating until stiff peaks form and SPLENDA® Sugar Blend dissolves. Spread meringue evenly over chocolate filling.

4. Bake 2 hours. Turn oven off and leave in oven, with door closed and oven light on for 8 hours or overnight.

Per serving: calories 340 (calories from fat 130), protein 5g, fat 14g (saturated fat 6g), carbohydrates 46g, fiber 3g, cholesterol 0mg, sodium 190mg, sugar 37g
Dietary exchanges: 3 starches, 3 fats

Banana Strawberry Shake

Prep Time:
5 minutes
Total Time:
5 minutes

**Makes
2 servings**

1 **large ripe banana,
   sliced**

5 **packets SPLENDA® No
   Calorie Sweetener**

½ **cup reduced-fat milk**

1¼ **cups frozen
   unsweetened
   strawberries**

1. Combine all ingredients in the jar of a blender.
Blend on medium speed until smooth.

2. Pour into glasses and serve.

Per serving: calories 140 (calories from fat 15), protein 3g, fat 2g
(saturated fat 1g), carbohydrates 31g, fiber 5g, cholesterol 5mg,
sodium 35mg, sugar 25g
Dietary exchanges: 2 fruits

Peanut Butter and Jelly Bites

Peanut Butter Balls:

1. **packet SPLENDA® No Calorie Sweetener Flavors for Coffee, Caramel**

1. **packet SPLENDA® No Calorie Sweetener Flavors for Coffee, French Vanilla**

1. **tablespoon sugar-free cocoa mix**

1. **tablespoon graham cracker crumbs**

2. **tablespoons peanut butter**

1½ **teaspoons fat-free cream cheese**

Garnish:

2. **tablespoons graham cracker crumbs**

2. **teaspoons sugar-free or no-sugar-added jam**

Prep Time:
10 minutes

Total Time:
10 minutes

**Makes
2 servings**

1. Mix all peanut butter ball ingredients together in a small bowl. Roll into 6 balls. Roll balls in graham cracker crumbs.

2. Press a small indentation in center with fingertip. Fill with jelly. Serve immediately.

Per serving: calories 150 (calories from fat 80), protein 6g, fat 9g (saturated fat 2g), carbohydrates 15g, fiber 1g, cholesterol 0mg, sodium 170mg, sugar 5g
Dietary exchanges: 1 starch, 1½ fats

Sweet and Spicy Snack Mix

Prep Time:
10 minutes

Cook Time:
25 minutes

Total Time:
35 minutes

**Makes
16 servings**

3 cups crispy rice cereal squares

2 cups toasted O-shaped cereal

2 cups small reduced-fat pretzels

1 cup oyster crackers

1 cup dry roasted peanuts

1 egg white

½ cup SPLENDA® No Calorie Sweetener, Granulated

1 tablespoon Worcestershire sauce

½ teaspoon ground red pepper

1. Preheat oven to 300°F.

2. Combine first 5 ingredients in a large bowl.

3. Beat egg white until foamy; stir in SPLENDA® Granulated Sweetener, Worcestershire sauce, and red pepper. Pour over cereal mixture, tossing to coat.

4. Spray a 15×10-inch jellyroll pan with nonstick cooking spray; spread cereal mixture in a single layer in pan.

5. Bake for 20–25 minutes, stirring every 10 minutes. Cool.

Per serving: calories 140 (calories from fat 50), protein 4g, fat 6g (saturated fat 1g), carbohydrates 17g, fiber 2g, cholesterol 0mg, sodium 300mg, sugar 1g
Dietary exchanges: 1 starch, 1 fat

Triple Grape KOOL-AID®
Brain Freeze

2 cups ice cubes

½ cup SPLENDA® No Calorie Sweetener, Granulated

2 (.13-ounce) envelopes KOOL-AID® Grape Flavor Unsweetened Soft Drink Mix

2 cups red seedless grapes, frozen*

1½ cups unsweetened purple grape juice

*To freeze grapes, individually remove them from the stems, wash thoroughly, and blot dry. Place in zip-top plastic bags and freeze to have ready whenever you need them.

Prep Time:
5 minutes
Total Time:
5 minutes

**Makes
4 servings**

Combine all ingredients in a blender in the order listed; process mixture until smooth, stopping to scrape down sides.

Per serving: calories 120 (calories from fat 5), protein 1g, fat 1g (saturated fat 0g), carbohydrates 28g, fiber 1g, cholesterol 0mg, sodium 45mg, sugar 28g
Dietary exchanges: 1 starch, 1 fruit

Banana Mini-Chip Muffins

Prep Time:
10 minutes

Cook Time:
20 minutes

Total Time:
40 minutes

**Makes
48 servings**

2 cups all-purpose flour

2 teaspoons baking
powder

½ teaspoon salt

¾ cup light butter,
softened

⅓ cup SPLENDA® Sugar
Blend

⅓ cup packed
SPLENDA® Brown
Sugar Blend

1 teaspoon vanilla
extract

3 medium ripe
bananas, mashed

1 large egg

1 (12-ounce) package
NESTLE® TOLL
HOUSE® Semi-Sweet
Chocolate Mini
Morsels

1. Preheat oven to 350°F. Spray 48 mini muffin cups
with nonstick cooking spray; set aside.

2. Combine flour, baking powder, and salt in medium
bowl; set aside.

3. Combine butter, SPLENDA® Sugar Blend, SPLENDA®
Brown Sugar Blend, and vanilla in large bowl; beat
at medium speed with a mixer until creamy. Beat in
bananas and egg. Gradually mix in flour mixture; stir in
morsels. Spoon batter evenly into prepared pan, filling
cups ⅔ full.

4. Bake 15–20 minutes or until wooden pick inserted in
center comes out clean. Cool 10 minutes in pans on
wire rack. Remove muffins from pans to wire rack to
cool completely.

Per serving: calories 90 (calories from fat 35), protein 1g, fat 4g
(saturated fat 2g), carbohydrates 13g, fiber 0g, cholesterol 10mg,
sodium 55mg, sugar 8g
Dietary exchanges: 1 starch, ½ fat

KOOL-AID® Fizzy Float

Prep Time:
10 minutes

Total Time:
10 minutes

**Makes
8 servings**

1 **quart cold water**

2 **cups light white grape juice, chilled**

1 **cup SPLENDA® No Calorie Sweetener, Granulated**

1 **envelope your favorite flavor KOOL-AID® Unsweetened Soft Drink Mix**

2 **cups seltzer water, chilled**

2 **cups no-sugar-added light vanilla ice cream**

1. Combine water, grape juice, SPLENDA® Granulated Sweetener, and KOOL-AID® Soft Drink Mix in a pitcher, stirring until SPLENDA® Granulated Sweetener dissolves.

2. Pour ¾ cup of the mixture into each of 8 tall glasses; add ¼ cup of the seltzer to each glass. Top each serving with ¼ cup of the ice cream. Serve immediately. Store leftover prepared drink in refrigerator.

Per serving: calories 70 (calories from fat 20), protein 1g, fat 2g (saturated fat 1g), carbohydrates 15g, fiber 0g, cholesterol 5mg, sodium 40mg, sugar 7g
Dietary exchanges: 1 starch

Strawberry Orange Smash Smoothie

Prep Time:
10 minutes

Total Time:
10 minutes

**Makes
5 servings**

3 cups frozen
strawberries,
unsweetened

⅔ cup SPLENDA® No
Calorie Sweetener,
Granulated

1¼ cups orange juice,
calcium fortified

1 cup fat-free,
plain yogurt

½ teaspoon vanilla
extract

¼ cup ice cubes

Add all ingredients to blender. Blender will be full.
Mix on low speed for 10 seconds. Remove lid, stir
with wooden spoon. Mix on medium speed for 15–20
seconds, remove lid and stir again. Mix on high speed
for 15–20 seconds or until smooth. Pour into glasses.
Serve immediately.

Per serving: calories 80 (calories from fat 0), protein 3g, fat 0g
(saturated fat 0g), carbohydrates 19g, fiber 2g, cholesterol 0mg,
sodium 30mg, sugar 14g
Dietary exchanges: 1 fruit

Deliciously Simple Applesauce

3 pounds apples, peeled, cored, and chopped

3 cups water

¼ cup SPLENDA® No Calorie Sweetener, Granulated

1 tablespoon lemon juice

1 teaspoon ground cinnamon

Prep Time:
15 minutes

Cook Time:
25 minutes

Total Time:
40 minutes

Makes 8 servings

1. Place apples in a large saucepan and just barely cover with water. Simmer over medium-low heat until apples are tender, 15–20 minutes.

2. Run cooked apples through a food mill or blender. Stir in the SPLENDA® Granulated Sweetener, lemon juice, and cinnamon. Cook over medium heat for about 3–5 minutes.

Per serving: calories 100 (calories from fat 5), protein 0g, fat 1g (saturated fat 0g), carbohydrates 26g, fiber 5g, cholesterol 0mg, sodium 0mg, sugar 20g
Dietary exchanges: 1½ fruits

Favorite Bites and Bars

Just-Like-Mom's Chocolate Chip Cookies

Prep Time:
15 minutes

Cook Time:
11 minutes

Total Time:
26 minutes

**Makes
36 servings**

2¼ cups all-purpose flour

1 teaspoon baking soda

1 teaspoon salt

1 cup butter or margarine

½ cup SPLENDA® Sugar Blend

½ cup firmly packed light brown sugar

1 teaspoon vanilla extract

2 large eggs

1 (12-ounce) package semi-sweet chocolate morsels

1. Preheat oven to 375°F.

2. Combine flour, baking soda, and salt in a small bowl. Set aside.

3. Beat butter, SPLENDA® Sugar Blend, brown sugar, and vanilla at medium speed with an electric mixer until blended. Add eggs, one at a time, mixing well after each addition. Scrape sides of bowl. Gradually add flour mixture, beating until blended. Stir in chocolate morsels.

4. Spoon rounded tablespoons of cookie dough onto ungreased baking sheets.

5. Bake cookies 9–11 minutes or until lightly browned. Remove from oven and cool on a wire rack.

Per serving: calories 150 (calories from fat 70), protein 2g, fat 8g (saturated fat 5g), carbohydrates 18g, fiber 1g, cholesterol 25mg, sodium 160mg, sugar 11g
Dietary exchanges: 1 starch, 1½ fats

Penuche Candy Squares

Prep Time:
20 minutes

Cook Time:
20 minutes

Total Time:
1 hour,
30 minutes

**Makes
16 servings**

¾ **cup SPLENDA® Sugar Blend**

1 **cup firmly packed brown sugar**

⅓ **cup half and half**

⅓ **cup 2% reduced-fat milk**

2 **tablespoons butter**

1 **teaspoon vanilla extract**

½ **cup chopped pecans**

1. Grease an 8×8-inch pan with nonstick cooking spray.

2. Butter sides of a heavy 2-quart saucepan; add SPLENDA® Sugar Blend, brown sugar, half and half, and milk. Cook over medium-high heat until mixture comes to a boil. Reduce heat to medium-low and cook, stirring frequently, until candy thermometer reaches 236°F. or soft ball stage (about 15–20 minutes). Remove from heat. Add butter and vanilla; do not stir. Cool, without stirring, until mixture reaches 110°F. (about 50 minutes).

3. Add pecans; beat with a wooden spoon or with a mixer fitted with paddle attachment until mixture thickens and just begins to lose its gloss. Quickly pour into prepared pan and spread evenly. Score in squares and cool completely; cut when firm.

Per serving: calories 150 (calories from fat 45), protein 1g, fat 5g (saturated fat 2g), carbohydrates 23g, fiber 0g, cholesterol 5mg, sodium 25mg, sugar 23g
Dietary exchanges: 1½ starches, 1 fat

Blueberry Cheesecake Bars

Prep Time:
15 minutes

Cook Time:
40 minutes

Total Time:
3 hours,
25 minutes

**Makes
20 servings**

Crust:

1¼ **cups graham cracker crumbs**

¼ **cup SPLENDA® No Calorie Sweetener, Granulated**

⅓ **cup light butter, melted**

Filling:

12 **ounces reduced-fat cream cheese, softened**

⅔ **cup SPLENDA® No Calorie Sweetener, Granulated**

2 **large eggs**

⅓ **cup reduced-fat sour cream**

2 **teaspoons vanilla extract**

¾ **cup fresh or frozen blueberries**

Topping:

¼ **cup reduced-sugar apricot preserves**

1 **tablespoon water**

1. Preheat oven to 350°F. Spray an 8×8-inch square pan with nonstick cooking spray. Set aside.

2. Combine graham cracker crumbs, SPLENDA® Granulated Sweetener, and butter, mixing well. Firmly press mixture evenly in bottom of prepared pan. Bake 5 minutes. Remove from oven; set aside.

3. Beat cream cheese at medium speed with an electric mixer until smooth. Gradually add SPLENDA® Granulated Sweetener, beating until blended. Add eggs, one at a time, beating well after each addition. Add sour cream and vanilla, beating just until blended. Gently stir in blueberries. Pour mixture into prepared pan.

4. Bake for 30–35 minutes, or until firm. Remove from oven and cool on a wire rack for 30 minutes. Cover and chill 2 hours.

5. Topping Directions: Combine apricot preserves and water in a small saucepan. Cook over medium heat, stirring constantly until jam melts. Spread over filling; cut into bars.

Per serving: calories 100 (calories from fat 60), protein 3g, fat 6g (saturated fat 3g), carbohydrates 7g, fiber 0g, cholesterol 40mg, sodium 110mg, sugar 3g
Dietary exchanges: *½ starch, 1 fat*

Angel Bites

5 egg whites

⅓ cup SPLENDA® No Calorie Sweetener, Granulated

1½ teaspoons vanilla

1 pinch salt

Prep Time:
20 minutes

Cook Time:
15 minutes

Total Time:
35 minutes

**Makes
5 servings**

1. Preheat oven to 350°F. Lightly oil a 13×11-inch baking sheet. Set aside.

2. Make Angel Bites. Place egg whites in a medium mixing bowl. Whip on high speed using an electric mixer or wire whisk until frothy.

3. Add SPLENDA® Granulated Sweetener, vanilla, and salt. Mix on high speed until medium-stiff peaks form (approximately 20–30 seconds with an electric mixer).

4. Spoon rounded tablespoons of egg whites onto prepared baking sheet. Bake in preheated oven 10–15 minutes or until golden brown. Remove from pan. Cool.

5. Assemble Angel Bites. Just before serving, sandwich Angel Bites with filling of choice. Place filling on the bottom of one Angel Bite and top with another so that the bottoms of the Angel Bites are facing each other and the filling is sandwiched between them. Repeat with remaining Angel Bites.

Per serving: calories 20 (calories from fat 0), protein 4g, fat 0g (saturated fat 0g), carbohydrates 1g, fiber 0g, cholesterol 0mg, sodium 130mg, sugar 0g
Dietary exchanges: ½ lean meat

Crispy-Chewy Oatmeal Raisin Cookies

Prep Time:
15 minutes

Cook Time:
12 minutes

Total Time:
27 minutes

**Makes
36 servings**

1½ **cups all-purpose flour**

1 **teaspoon baking soda**

1 **teaspoon ground cinnamon**

1 **cup butter, softened**

1 **cup SPLENDA® Sugar Blend**

2 **large eggs**

1 **tablespoon molasses**

1½ **teaspoons vanilla extract**

3 **cups old-fashioned oatmeal, uncooked**

1 **cup raisins**

1. Preheat oven to 350°F.

2. Stir together flour, soda, and cinnamon. Set aside.

3. Beat butter and SPLENDA® Sugar Blend at medium speed with an electric mixer until fluffy. Add eggs, molasses, and vanilla, beating until blended. Gradually add flour mixture, beating at low speed until blended.

4. Stir in oats and raisins.

5. Drop dough by rounded tablespoons onto lightly greased baking sheets.

6. Bake 10–12 minutes or until lightly browned. Cool slightly on baking sheets. Remove to wire racks; cool completely.

Per serving: calories 140 (calories from fat 50), protein 2g, fat 6g (saturated fat 3g), carbohydrates 18g, fiber 1g, cholesterol 25mg, sodium 90mg, sugar 9g
Dietary exchanges: 1 starch, 1 fat

Chocolate Chip Meringue Crisps

Prep Time:
15 minutes

Cook Time:
2 hours,
5 minutes

Total Time:
2 hours,
20 minutes

**Makes
36 servings**

½ **cup chopped
walnuts**

2 **egg whites**

½ **teaspoon vanilla
extract**

½ **cup SPLENDA® Sugar
Blend**

½ **cup semi-sweet
chocolate morsels**

1. Preheat oven to 200°F.

2. Bake walnuts in a shallow pan, stirring occasionally,
5 minutes or until toasted. Set aside.

3. Beat egg whites and vanilla at high speed with an
electric mixer until foamy.

4. Add SPLENDA® Sugar Blend, 1 tablespoon at a
time, beating until stiff peaks form; stir in walnuts and
chocolate morsels.

5. Spoon rounded teaspoons of mixture on baking
sheets lined with parchment paper.

6. Bake 2 hours. Cool slightly on cookie sheet. Remove
to wire racks to cool completely. Store in an airtight tin.

Per serving: calories 35 (calories from fat 15), protein 1g, fat 2g
(saturated fat 1g), carbohydrates 4g, fiber 0g, cholesterol 0mg,
sodium 0mg, sugar 4g
Dietary exchanges: ½ starch

Harvest Pumpkin-Oatmeal Raisin Cookies

Prep Time:
15 minutes

Cook Time:
16 minutes

Total Time:
31 minutes

**Makes
48 servings**

- 2 cups all-purpose flour
- 1⅓ cups quick or old-fashioned oats
- 1 teaspoon baking soda
- 1 teaspoon ground cinnamon
- ½ teaspoon salt
- 1 cup butter or margarine, softened
- ½ cup SPLENDA® Sugar Blend
- ½ cup SPLENDA® Brown Sugar Blend, packed
- 1 cup LIBBY'S® 100% Pure Pumpkin
- 1 large egg
- 1 teaspoon vanilla extract
- ¾ cup chopped walnuts
- ¾ cup raisins

1. Preheat oven to 350°F. Spray baking sheets with nonstick cooking spray; set aside.

2. Combine flour, oats, baking soda, cinnamon, and salt in medium bowl. Beat butter, SPLENDA® Sugar Blend, and SPLENDA® Brown Sugar Blend in large bowl at medium speed until light and fluffy. Add pumpkin, egg, and vanilla; mix well. Add flour mixture; mix well. Stir in walnuts and raisins. Drop by rounded tablespoons onto prepared baking sheets.

3. Bake 14–16 minutes or until cookies are lightly browned and set in centers. Cool on baking sheets for 2 minutes; remove to wire racks to cool completely.

Per serving: calories 110 (calories from fat 50), protein 2g, fat 5g (saturated fat 3g), carbohydrates 12g, fiber 1g, cholesterol 15mg, sodium 90mg, sugar 6g
Dietary exchanges: 1 starch, 1 fat

Apple Cookies

Prep Time:
15 minutes

Cook Time:
12 minutes

Total Time:
27 minutes

**Makes
30 servings**

¾ **cup butter, softened**

1 **cup SPLENDA® No
Calorie Sweetener,
Granulated**

2 **teaspoons freshly
grated lemon peel**

2 **teaspoons molasses**

2 **large eggs**

½ **cup unsweetened
applesauce**

⅓ **cup apple juice
concentrate**

1¾ **cups all-purpose flour**

⅔ **cup old-fashioned
oats**

1 **teaspoon baking
soda**

1½ **teaspoons ground
cinnamon**

⅛ **teaspoon ground
nutmeg**

1 **cup diced fresh
apples**

½ **cup raisins**

1. Preheat oven to 325°F. Lightly spray baking sheets with nonstick cooking spray.

2. Beat butter, SPLENDA® Granulated Sweetener, lemon peel, and molasses on high speed with an electric mixer 1 minute. Add eggs, one at a time, beating just until yellow disappears after each addition.

3. Combine applesauce and apple juice concentrate; set aside.

4. Combine flour, oats, soda, cinnamon, and nutmeg. Gradually add to butter mixture alternately with applesauce mixture, beginning and ending with flour mixture, beating at low speed until blended after each addition. Stir in apples and raisins.

5. Drop by tablespoonfuls, 1½ inches apart, onto prepared baking sheets.

6. Bake 10–12 minutes. Cool on wire racks.

Per serving: calories 100 (calories from fat 45), protein 2g, fat 5g (saturated fat 3g), carbohydrates 12g, fiber 1g, cholesterol 25mg, sodium 95mg, sugar 4g
Dietary exchanges: 1 starch, 1 fat

Chunky Peanut Butter Triangles

Prep Time:
10 minutes

Cook Time:
20 minutes

Total Time:
30 minutes

**Makes
42 servings**

1½ cups all-purpose flour

½ teaspoon baking soda

¾ cup creamy or chunky peanut butter

½ cup light butter, softened

¼ cup SPLENDA® Sugar Blend

⅓ cup packed SPLENDA® Brown Sugar Blend

1 large egg

1 teaspoon vanilla extract

1 (11.5-ounce) package NESTLE® TOLL HOUSE® Semi-Sweet Chocolate Chunks

1. Preheat oven to 350°F.

2. Combine flour and baking soda in small bowl; set aside.

3. Combine peanut butter, butter, SPLENDA® Sugar Blend, and SPLENDA® Brown Sugar Blend in large bowl; beat at medium speed until creamy. Beat in egg and vanilla. Gradually beat in flour mixture. Stir in chocolate chunks. Press into ungreased 13×9-inch baking pan, distributing chocolate chunks evenly.

4. Bake 18–20 minutes or until center is set. Cool completely in pan on wire rack. Cut into bars; slice each bar in half diagonally.

Per serving: calories 110 (calories from fat 50), protein 2g, fat 6g (saturated fat 3g), carbohydrates 12g, fiber 1g, cholesterol 10mg, sodium 50mg, sugar 8g
Dietary exchanges: 1 starch, 1 fat

Almond Cheesecake Bars

Prep Time:
15 minutes

Cook Time:
59 minutes

Total Time:
1 hour,
14 minutes

**Makes
20 servings**

Crust:

¼ **cup SPLENDA® No Calorie Sweetener, Granulated**

1¼ **cups graham cracker or vanilla wafer crumbs**

⅓ **cup light butter, melted**

¼ **cup toasted sliced almonds, finely ground**

Filling:

12 **ounces reduced-fat cream cheese**

½ **cup SPLENDA® No Calorie Sweetener, Granulated**

2 **large eggs**

¼ **cup reduced-fat sour cream**

2½ **teaspoons vanilla extract**

1 **teaspoon almond extract**

¼ **cup toasted, sliced almonds**

1. Preheat oven to 350°F.

2. Spray one 8×8-inch square pan with nonstick cooking spray. Set aside.

3. Mix crust ingredients together in a mixing bowl. Mix well. Press into prepared pan. Bake 10–12 minutes or until firm.

3. Mix cream cheese and SPLENDA® Granulated Sweetener together until smooth. Add eggs, one at a time, scraping the sides of the bowl, and mixing well after each addition. Add sour cream and extracts; mix well. Pour over prepared crust.

4. Bake in preheated oven for 40–47 minutes, or until firm.

5. Top with toasted almonds.

Per serving: calories 110 (calories from fat 70), protein 4g, fat 8g (saturated fat 4g), carbohydrates 7g, fiber 0g, cholesterol 35mg, sodium 105mg, sugar 3g
Dietary exchanges: ½ starch, 1½ fats

Sweet and Simple Desserts

Fresh Strawberry Pie

Prep Time:
20 minutes

Total Time:
50 minutes

**Makes
8 servings**

¹⁄₃ **cup water**

1 **cup SPLENDA® No Calorie Sweetener, Granulated**

1 **(1-ounce) package unflavored gelatin**

¹⁄₃ **cup water**

6 **cups strawberries, cleaned and cut in half**

1 **(9-inch) prepared reduced-fat graham cracker crust**

1. Pour ¹⁄₃ cup water in a small mixing bowl. Add SPLENDA® Granulated Sweetener. Stir well. Sprinkle gelatin over the top. Let stand 1 minute.

2. Pour ¹⁄₃ cup water in a small pan. Boil. Pour boiling water over gelatin mixture. Stir until dissolved.

3. Refrigerate approximately 20 minutes or until the mixture begins to thicken. Stir frequently.

4. Toss with prepared berries and spoon into pie crust. Chill until set.

Per serving: *calories 140 (calories from fat 35), protein 5g, fat 4g (saturated fat 1g), carbohydrates 22g, fiber 3g, cholesterol 0mg, sodium 95mg, sugar 6g*
Dietary exchanges: *½ starch, 1 fruit, 1 fat*

Chocolate Velvet Mousse

Prep Time:
25 minutes

Total Time:
8 hours,
25 minutes

**Makes
6 servings**

3 ounces unsweetened chocolate

1 cup low-fat milk

¼ cup egg substitute

½ cup SPLENDA® No Calorie Sweetener, Granulated

1 teaspoon cornstarch

2 tablespoons orange-flavored liqueur or brandy*

½ cup heavy cream

3 cups sliced strawberries

*For dietary purposes, please note that this recipe contains alcohol. Alcohol can be replaced with 1 teaspoon orange extract.

1. Place chocolate and milk in a medium saucepan. Heat over medium heat until chocolate melts. Set aside.

2. Stir together egg substitute, SPLENDA® Granulated Sweetener, cornstarch, and orange-flavored liqueur or brandy in a small mixing bowl. Add to chocolate mixture. Stir constantly. Cook over medium heat while stirring constantly, until mixture begins to thicken (approximately 3–4 minutes). Remove from heat and pour into the bowl of a blender or food processor. Blend or process briefly (10–20 seconds) to make a more creamy texture. Pour into medium bowl and cover.

3. Refrigerate chocolate mixture approximately 2–3 hours or until cool. Whip cream until stiff and fold into chocolate. Refrigerate overnight to set. Mousse will keep refrigerated for 3 days.

4. To serve, layer strawberries and mousse in 6 all-purpose wine glasses.

Per serving: calories 210 (calories from fat 150), protein 5g, fat 17g (saturated fat 10g), carbohydrates 14g, fiber 4g, cholesterol 30mg, sodium 50mg, sugar 5g
Dietary exchanges: 1 starch, 3 fats

Nostalgic Apple Pie

Prep Time:
15 minutes

Cook Time:
50 minutes

Total Time:
1 hour,
5 minutes

**Makes
8 servings**

1 (15-ounce) package refrigerated pie crusts

7 cups baking apples, thin-sliced, cored, and peeled

1 cup SPLENDA® No Calorie Sweetener, Granulated

3 tablespoons cornstarch

¾ teaspoon ground cinnamon

¼ teaspoon ground nutmeg

⅛ teaspoon salt

1. Preheat oven to 425°F.

2. Unfold 1 pie crust; press out fold lines. Fit pie crust into a 9-inch pie plate according to package directions.

3. Place sliced apples into a large mixing bowl and set aside. Combine SPLENDA® Granulated Sweetener, cornstarch, cinnamon, nutmeg, and salt in a small bowl. Sprinkle mixture over apples and toss. Spoon apple mixture into pie crust. Place the second crust over the filling. Seal edges, trim, and flute. Make small openings in the top crust.

4. Bake in preheated oven 40–50 minutes or until the top crust is golden. Serve warm or chilled.

Per serving: calories 300 (calories from fat 140), protein 3g, fat 15g (saturated fat 4g), carbohydrates 40g, fiber 5g, cholesterol 0mg, sodium 270mg, sugar 14g

Dietary exchanges: 1½ starches, 1 fruit, 3 fats

'Nuts and Berries'

Prep Time:
5 minutes
Total Time:
5 minutes

**Makes
8 servings**

2 packets SPLENDA® No Calorie Sweetener Flavors for Coffee, Hazelnut

1 cup sugar-free nondairy topping

3 cups sliced strawberries

1 cup raspberries

Garnish:

   Fresh mint (optional)

1. Mix SPLENDA® Flavors for Coffee with nondairy topping. Set aside.

2. Toss berries together and place in serving dishes. Top with nondairy topping and a sprig of fresh mint, if desired.

Per serving: calories 50 (calories from fat 15), protein 1g, fat 1g (saturated fat 1g), carbohydrates 10g, fiber 2g, cholesterol 0mg, sodium 0mg, sugar 1g
Dietary exchanges: ½ fruit

Frozen Mini Cinnamon Coffee Cheesecakes

12 **NABISCO® Ginger Snaps**

2 tablespoons **MAXWELL HOUSE® Naturally Decaffeinated Instant Coffee**

1 tablespoon water

½ cup **SPLENDA® No Calorie Sweetener, Granulated**

1 (8-ounce) container **PHILADELPHIA® Light Cream Cheese Spread**

1 teaspoon vanilla

¼ teaspoon ground cinnamon

1½ cups thawed **COOL WHIP® Whipped Topping**

1 cup fresh raspberries

1. Line 12 muffin cups with paper liners. Place 1 cookie in each paper cup. Set aside.

2. Mix coffee granules and water in large bowl until coffee is dissolved. Add SPLENDA® Granulated Sweetener, cream cheese spread, vanilla, and cinnamon. Beat with wire whisk until well blended. Gently stir in whipped topping.

3. Spoon evenly over cookies in muffin pan. Top each cheesecake evenly with raspberries. Cover and freeze for 3 hours or overnight.

4. Remove from freezer about 10 minutes before serving to soften slightly.

Per serving: calories 35 (calories from fat 0), protein 0g, fat 2g (saturated fat 2g), carbohydrates 3g, fiber 1g, cholesterol 0mg, sodium 0mg, sugar 2g
Dietary exchanges: ½ starch

Apple Cranberry Pie

Prep Time:
30 minutes

Cook Time:
50 minutes

Total Time:
1 hour,
20 minutes

**Makes
8 servings**

1 **(15-ounce) package refrigerated pie crusts**

½ **cup SPLENDA® No Calorie Sweetener, Granulated**

1 **tablespoon all-purpose flour**

½ **teaspoon ground cinnamon**

4 **large Granny Smith apples, peeled, cored, and sliced**

1 **cup cranberries, coarsely chopped**

1. Preheat oven to 400°F.

2. Unfold 1 pie crust; press out fold lines. Fit pie crust into a 9-inch pie plate according to package directions.

3. Combine SPLENDA® Granulated Sweetener, flour, and cinnamon in a large bowl; add apples and cranberries, tossing gently. Spoon mixture into pie crust.

4. Unfold remaining pie crust; press out fold lines. Roll to ⅛-inch thickness. Place over filling; fold edges under and crimp. Cut slits in top to allow steam to escape.

5. Bake 40–50 minutes or until crust is golden. Cover edges with aluminum foil to prevent overbrowning, if necessary. Cool on a wire rack 1 hour before serving.

Per serving: calories 290 (calories from fat 130), protein 2g, fat 14g (saturated fat 6g), carbohydrates 41g, fiber 3g, cholesterol 10mg, sodium 200mg, sugar 13g
Dietary exchanges: 1½ starches, 1 fruit, 3 fats

Candied Walnut-Topped Pumpkin Pie

Prep Time:
20 minutes

Cook Time:
68 minutes

Total Time:
1 hour,
28 minutes

**Makes
8 servings**

1¼ cups coarsely
   chopped walnuts

⅓ cup SPLENDA® Brown
   Sugar Blend, packed

1 (9-inch) deep-dish
   pie shell

1 (15-ounce) can
   LIBBY'S® 100% Pure
   Pumpkin

1 (12-fluid-ounce) can
   NESTLE® CARNATION®
   Evaporated Milk

⅓ cup SPLENDA®
   Sugar Blend

2 large eggs, lightly
   beaten

1½ teaspoons pumpkin
   pie spice

¼ teaspoon salt

3 teaspoons butter,
   melted

1. Preheat oven to 425°F.

2. Combine walnuts and SPLENDA® Brown Sugar Blend in small bowl. Place ¾ cup of walnut mixture in pie shell. Combine pumpkin, evaporated milk, SPLENDA® Sugar Blend, eggs, pumpkin pie spice, and salt in medium bowl; mix well. Pour batter over nuts.

3. Bake 15 minutes. Reduce oven temperature to 350°F.; bake 40–50 minutes longer or until knife inserted near center comes out clean. Cool on wire rack.

4. Combine butter and remaining walnut mixture; stir until moistened. Sprinkle over cooled pie. Broil about 5 inches from heat for 2–3 minutes or until bubbly. Cool before serving.

Per serving: calories 410 (calories from fat 220), protein 9g, fat 24g (saturated fat 7g), carbohydrates 38g, fiber 4g, cholesterol 70mg, sodium 300mg, sugar 23g
Dietary exchanges: 2½ starches, 5 fats

Sweet Potato Cheesecake with Graham Cracker Crust

1¼ cups graham cracker crumbs

¼ cup butter, melted

2 pounds orange-fleshed sweet potatoes

3 (8-ounce) containers fat-free cream cheese, softened

½ cup SPLENDA® No Calorie Sweetener, Granulated

⅓ cup nonfat sour cream

¼ cup fat-free half and half

3 eggs

1 teaspoon ground cinnamon

½ teaspoon ground nutmeg

Prep Time:
20 minutes

Cook Time:
2 hours, 10 minutes

Total Time:
3 hours, 30 minutes

Makes 12 servings

1. Preheat oven to 350°F. Mix together graham cracker crumbs and melted butter. Press mixture into the bottom of a 9½-inch springform pan. Bake 10 minutes. Cool. Don't turn the oven off.

2. Place potatoes in a baking dish. Bake until a knife inserted in center goes through easily, about 1 hour. Don't turn oven off. Cool sweet potatoes enough to handle, peel, and purée.

3. Transfer 1½ cups of sweet potato purée to a large bowl. Mix in cream cheese, SPLENDA® Granulated Sweetener, sour cream, and half and half; beat until smooth. Beat in eggs one at a time, blending well after each. Season with cinnamon and nutmeg. Pour filling into crust.

4. Bake until tester inserted in center comes out clean, 1 hour. Turn off the oven. Let cake stand 1 hour in oven with door ajar. Cool to room temperature, and refrigerate to chill.

Per serving: calories 230 (calories from fat 60), protein 12g, fat 7g (saturated fat 3g), carbohydrates 30g, fiber 3g, cholesterol 70mg, sodium 440mg, sugar 7g
Dietary exchanges: 2 starches, 1 medium-fat meat

Berry-Cherry Pie

Prep Time:
25 minutes

Cook Time:
45 minutes

Total Time:
1 hour,
10 minutes

**Makes
8 servings**

1 **(15-ounce) package refrigerated pie crusts**

1 **(14.5-ounce) can pitted tart red cherries, undrained**

1 **(12-ounce) package frozen raspberries, thawed**

1 **cup fresh blueberries or frozen blueberries, thawed**

1 **cup SPLENDA® No Calorie Sweetener, Granulated**

¼ **cup cornstarch**

2 **tablespoons butter**

Optional topping:

Frozen low-fat vanilla yogurt

1. Preheat oven to 375°F.

2. Unfold 1 pie crust; press out fold lines. Fit pie crust into a 9-inch pie plate according to package directions. Set aside.

3. Drain cherries, raspberries, and blueberries (if frozen), reserving 1 cup of the juices. Set berries and juice aside.

4. Combine SPLENDA® Granulated Sweetener and cornstarch in a medium saucepan; gradually stir in reserved juice. Cook over medium heat, stirring constantly, until mixture begins to boil. Boil 1 minute, stirring constantly. Stir in butter and reserved fruit. Cool slightly and spoon mixture into pie shell.

5. Unroll remaining pie crust; roll to ⅛-inch thickness: place over filling. Fold edges under and crimp. Cut slits in top to allow steam to escape.

6. Bake 40–45 minutes or until crust is golden. Cover edges with aluminum foil to prevent excessive browning, if necessary. Cool on a wire rack. Serve with a scoop of frozen low-fat vanilla yogurt, if desired.

Per serving: calories 330 (calories from fat 170), protein 4g, fat 19g (saturated fat 6g), carbohydrates 37g, fiber 4g, cholesterol 10mg, sodium 290mg, sugar 7g
Dietary exchanges: 1½ starches, 1 fruit, 4 fats

Refreshing Drinks and Smoothies

Mock Sangria

Prep Time:
5 minutes
Total Time:
5 minutes
Makes
1 serving

2 packets SPLENDA® No Calorie Sweetener FLAVOR ACCENTS™, Lemon

1 thin slice fresh lemon

2 thin slices fresh orange

1 cup alcohol-removed wine

3 thin slices fresh apple

Ice, as desired

Crush SPLENDA® FLAVOR ACCENTS™, and lemon and orange slices with a fork in a tall glass. Add wine and stir. Add apple slices and ice as desired. Serve immediately.

Per serving: calories 35 (calories from fat 0), protein 1g, fat 0g (saturated fat 0g), carbohydrates 10g, fiber 1g, cholesterol 0mg, sodium 25mg, sugar 7g
Dietary exchanges: ½ fruit

Mix Ahead Hot Cocoa Mix

Prep Time:
5 minutes

Total Time:
5 minutes

**Makes
22 servings**

1 **(9.6-ounce) box
instant nonfat dry
milk powder**

1¼ **cups SPLENDA® No
Calorie Sweetener,
Granulated**

⅔ **cup powdered
non-dairy coffee
creamer**

⅔ **cup Dutch process
cocoa**

1. Combine all ingredients in a large bowl, stirring well.
Store in an airtight container.

2. Combine ¼ cup Hot Cocoa Mix with ¾ cup boiling
water for an individual serving. Serve immediately.

Per serving: calories 70 (calories from fat 15), protein 5g, fat 1g
(saturated fat 1g), carbohydrates 9g, fiber 1g, cholesterol 0mg,
sodium 70mg, sugar 8g
Dietary exchanges: ½ starch, ½ fat

Caramel Apple Cider

1 **packet SPLENDA® No Calorie Sweetener Flavors for Coffee, Caramel**

2 **packets SPLENDA® No Calorie Sweetener Flavors for Coffee, Cinnamon Spice**

1 **cup apple cider or apple juice**

Prep Time:
5 Minutes
Total Time:
5 Minutes

**Makes
1 serving**

Mix all ingredients together in a large mug or coffee cup. Heat in microwave until warm. Serve immediately.

Per serving: calories 120 (calories from fat 0), protein 0g, fat 0g (saturated fat 0g), carbohydrates 32g, fiber 0g, cholesterol 0mg, sodium 25mg, sugar 26g
Dietary exchanges: 2 fruits

Hot Tea Punch

Prep Time:
10 minutes

Total Time:
10 minutes

**Makes
2 servings**

**3 packets SPLENDA® No
   Calorie Sweetener**

**1 (3-inch) cinnamon
   stick**

1 whole clove

1 cup water

2 tea bags

**½ cup fresh orange
   juice**

**2 teaspoons fresh
   lemon juice**

1. Bring first 4 ingredients to a boil in a heavy saucepan; boil 2 minutes. Remove from heat and add tea bags. Cover and steep for 5 minutes. Remove spices and tea bags with a slotted spoon.

2. Stir in juices. Serve immediately.

Per serving: calories 35, (calories from fat 0), protein 1g, fat 0g (saturated fat 0g), carbohydrates 9g, fiber 1g, cholesterol 0mg, sodium 5mg, sugar 7g
Dietary exchanges: *½ fruit*

Berry-Banana Smoothie

2 cups 1% low-fat milk

1 ripe banana, sliced

½ cup SPLENDA® No Calorie Sweetener, Granulated

1 (0.13-ounce) package KOOL-AID® Strawberry Flavor Unsweetened Soft Drink Mix

2 cups ice cubes

Prep Time: 5 Minutes

Total Time: 5 Minutes

Makes 4 servings

Process milk, banana, SPLENDA® Granulated Sweetener, KOOL-AID® Soft Drink Mix, and ice cubes in a blender until smooth, stopping to scrape down sides. Serve immediately.

Per serving: calories 80, (calories from fat 15), protein 4g, fat 1g (saturated fat 1g), carbohydrates 13g, fiber 1g, cholesterol 5mg, sodium 110mg, sugar 11g
Dietary exchanges: 1 starch

Banana Colada Smoothie

Prep Time:
5 minutes

Total Time:
5 minutes

**Makes
2 servings**

1 cup ice cubes

1 cup chopped fresh pineapple

1 small ripe banana, sliced

3 tablespoons SPLENDA® No Calorie Sweetener, Granulated

½ cup reduced-fat coconut milk

½ teaspoon vanilla extract

Combine all ingredients in a blender in the order listed; process mixture until smooth, stopping to scrape down sides.

Per serving: calories 140, (calories from fat 50), protein 1g, fat 6g (saturated fat 3g), carbohydrates 23g, fiber 2g, cholesterol 0mg, sodium 10mg, sugar 18g
Dietary exchanges: *1½ fruits, 1 fat*

Blackberry Twist Lemonade

2 cups fresh blackberries, or unsweetened frozen blackberries, thawed

1 cup fresh lemon juice

1 cup SPLENDA® No Calorie Sweetener, Granulated

4 cups cold water

Prep Time:
15 Minutes

Total Time:
15 Minutes

**Makes
7 servings**

Combine blackberries, lemon juice, and SPLENDA® Granulated Sweetener in a blender; process until smooth, stopping to scrape down sides. Press mixture through a sieve into a pitcher; discard solids. Stir in water. Serve over ice.

Per serving: calories 30, (calories from fat 0), protein 0g, fat 0g (saturated fat 0g), carbohydrates 8g, fiber 2g, cholesterol 0mg, sodium 0mg, sugar 4g
Dietary exchanges: ½ fruit

Citrus Berry Spritzer

Prep Time:
10 minutes

Total Time:
10 minutes

**Makes
1 serving**

2 teaspoons raspberry
or apple raspberry
juice concentrate

1 packet SPLENDA® No
Calorie Sweetener
FLAVOR ACCENTS™,
Lemon

1 packet SPLENDA® No
Calorie Sweetener
FLAVOR ACCENTS™,
Raspberry

½ cup seltzer or
sparkling mineral
water

½ cup orange juice

Ice, as desired

1. Thaw raspberry juice concentrate. Set aside.

2. Mix SPLENDA® FLAVOR ACCENTS™ into seltzer water.
Add orange juice.

3. Place ice in a tall clear glass. Pour juice mixture
into glass. Spoon juice concentrate on top. Serve
immediately.

Per serving: calories 80 (calories from fat 0), protein 1g, fat 0g
(saturated fat 0g), carbohydrates 21g, fiber 0g, cholesterol 0mg,
sodium 40mg, sugar 17g
Dietary exchanges: 1½ fruits

Chai Banana Smoothie

Prep Time:
25 minutes

Chill Time:
40 minutes

Total Time:
1 hour,
5 minutes

**Makes
4 servings**

4 **large bananas,
peeled and sliced**

1 **cup 1% low-fat milk**

1 **regular-size chai tea
bag**

⅓ **cup SPLENDA® No
Calorie Sweetener,
Granulated**

¾ **cup plain fat-free
yogurt**

1. Place bananas in freezer for about 30 minutes or until frozen.

2. Pour milk into a microwave-safe measuring cup; microwave at HIGH for 1 minute or just until milk boils; add chai tea bag and let steep for 20 minutes, pressing bag gently with a spoon to release chai flavor. Remove and discard tea bag; chill chai-flavored milk for 10 minutes.

3. Combine frozen bananas, SPLENDA® Granulated Sweetener, yogurt, and chai-flavored milk in a blender. Process mixture until smooth, stopping to scrape down sides.

Per serving: calories 180 (calories from fat 10), protein 6g, fat 1g (saturated fat 1g), carbohydrates 38g, fiber 3g, cholesterol 5mg, sodium 70mg, sugar 32g
Dietary exchanges: 2 fruits, ½ fat-free milk

Cool Mint and Orange Tea

Prep Time:
10 minutes

Total Time:
10 minutes

**Makes
10 servings**

12 sprigs fresh mint

4 tea bags

3 cups boiling water

¾ cup SPLENDA® No
  Calorie Sweetener,
  Granulated

1 cup orange juice

¼ cup lemon juice

5 cups cold water

3 orange slices for
  garnish (optional)

3 lemon slices for
  garnish (optional)

Place the mint sprigs and tea bags into a large pitcher. Pour boiling water over them, and allow to steep for about 8 minutes. Remove and discard the tea bags and mint leaves, squeezing out excess liquid. Stir in SPLENDA® Granulated Sweetener until dissolved, then stir in the orange and lemon juices. Pour in the cold water. Serve over ice cubes, and garnish with orange and lemon slices.

Per serving: calories 15 (calories from fat 0), protein 0g, fat 0g (saturated fat 0g), carbohydrates 4g, fiber 0g, cholesterol 0mg, sodium 5mg, sugar 3g
Dietary exchanges: free

Pineapple Pear Frosty

2 (8-ounce) cans crushed pineapple in its own juice

1 (15-ounce) can drained sliced pears in light syrup

1 cup plain fat-free yogurt

½ cup SPLENDA® No Calorie Sweetener, Granulated

½ teaspoon vanilla extract

Prep Time:
5 minutes

Total Time:
25 minutes

Makes
5 servings

1. Place pineapple and pears in freezer for 20 minutes or until frozen.

2. Process frozen pineapple and pears and remaining ingredients in a blender on low speed until smooth (blender will be full), stopping frequently to scrape sides down.

Per serving: calories 110 (calories from fat 0), protein 3g, fat 0g (saturated fat 0g), carbohydrates 25g, fiber 3g, cholesterol 0mg, sodium 40mg, sugar 18g
Dietary exchanges: 1½ fruits

Soothing Warm Milk

Prep Time:
1 minute

Cook Time:
2 minutes

Total Time:
3 minutes

**Makes
2 servings**

2 cups 1% low-fat milk

**2 teaspoons vanilla
extract**

**1 tablespoon
SPLENDA® No
Calorie Sweetener,
Granulated**

**½ teaspoon ground
nutmeg**

In 2 large mugs, stir together the milk, vanilla, and
SPLENDA® Granulated Sweetener. Heat in the
microwave on full power for 2 minutes. Stir in nutmeg,
and serve hot.

Per serving: calories 120, (calories from fat 25), protein 9g, fat 3g
(saturated fat 2g), carbohydrates 13g, fiber 0g, cholesterol 10mg,
sodium 130mg, sugar 0g
Dietary exchanges: 1 low-fat milk

index

METRIC CONVERSION CHART

VOLUME MEASUREMENTS (dry)

1/8 teaspoon = 0.5 mL
1/4 teaspoon = 1 mL
1/2 teaspoon = 2 mL
3/4 teaspoon = 4 mL
1 teaspoon = 5 mL
1 tablespoon = 15 mL
2 tablespoons = 30 mL
1/4 cup = 60 mL
1/3 cup = 75 mL
1/2 cup = 125 mL
2/3 cup = 150 mL
3/4 cup = 175 mL
1 cup = 250 mL
2 cups = 1 pint = 500 mL
3 cups = 750 mL
4 cups = 1 quart = 1 L

VOLUME MEASUREMENTS (fluid)

1 fluid ounce (2 tablespoons) = 30 mL
4 fluid ounces (1/2 cup) = 125 mL
8 fluid ounces (1 cup) = 250 mL
12 fluid ounces (1 1/2 cups) = 375 mL
16 fluid ounces (2 cups) = 500 mL

WEIGHTS (mass)

1/2 ounce = 15 g
1 ounce = 30 g
3 ounces = 90 g
4 ounces = 120 g
8 ounces = 225 g
10 ounces = 285 g
12 ounces = 360 g
16 ounces = 1 pound = 450 g

DIMENSIONS

1/16 inch = 2 mm
1/8 inch = 3 mm
1/4 inch = 6 mm
1/2 inch = 1.5 cm
3/4 inch = 2 cm
1 inch = 2.5 cm

OVEN TEMPERATURES

250°F = 120°C
275°F = 140°C
300°F = 150°C
325°F = 160°C
350°F = 180°C
375°F = 190°C
400°F = 200°C
425°F = 220°C
450°F = 230°C

BAKING PAN SIZES

Utensil	Size in Inches/Quarts	Metric Volume	Size in Centimeters
Baking or	8×8×2	2 L	20×20×5
Cake Pan	9×9×2	2.5 L	23×23×5
(square or	12×8×2	3 L	30×20×5
rectangular)	13×9×2	3.5 L	33×23×5
Loaf Pan	8×4×3	1.5 L	20×10×7
	9×5×3	2 L	23×13×7
Round Layer	8×1½	1.2 L	20×4
Cake Pan	9×1½	1.5 L	23×4
Pie Plate	8×1¼	750 mL	20×3
	9×1¼	1 L	23×3
Baking Dish	1 quart	1 L	—
or Casserole	1½ quarts	1.5 L	—
	2 quarts	2 L	—